THE STORYTELLER

by CLAUDIA MYERS

The Storyteller

Copyright © 2023 Claudia Myers

All rights reserved. No part of this book may be reproduced or utilized in any form or by any means, electronic or mechanical, including photocopying, recording, or by any information storage or retrieval system, without permission in writing from the publisher.

Published by:

Confections

www.claudiamyersdesigns.com

ISBN: 979-8-218-18183-3

Printed in Duluth Minnesota, U.S.A. By JS Print Group

10 9 8 7 6 5 4 3 2 1

My thanks to Voula and Jim Heffernan, Beverly Godfrey (my first editor), Katie Rohman (my current editor), and to the Editorial Board of the Duluth News Tribune for allowing me to reprint my columns. And of course, thanks to my husband, Tom Myers: proofreader, critic, and biggest fan.

Thanks to all on "my Friends and Fam list" for the constant stream of encouragement, and to those of you I do not know, but who have had the kindness to tell me you enjoy reading my column. It always surprises me.

Introduction

The first column that I had printed in the Duluth News Tribune was actually written as a New Year's letter to my friends. One of the people it was sent to is married to a long-time columnist with the DNT and after she shared it with him, he suggested sending it in to the newspaper. My first reaction was "No, I only meant it for my friends and family." The end, period. Then, my ego got the better of me and I thought, "Well, if he thinks it's good enough, maybe I'll give it a shot. And, what do you know, the editor liked it enough to not only print it, but invite me to continue to contribute a column every other Wednesday. And I discovered something about myself that I didn't know-- I love to write.

CONTENTS

1. The Year the World Took a Time-Out   page 4
2. The Stubborn Gardener   page 7
3. River's Bend   page 11
4. The Visitors   page 15
5. Fixing River's Bend   page 19
6. Freedom to Read   page 23
7. Go Big or Get Outta Here   page 28
8. Design Your Own Log House   page 32
9. Log House Adventure Run Amok   page 36
10. Here Fishie, Fishie   page 41
11. More Fish Tales   page 45
12. New and Improved   page 49
13. Disasters I Have Known   page 54
14. Whaddya Say?   page 58
15. Pets and Pets and Pets   page 63
16. It's All About the Dogs   page 68
17. Music Makes the Family Go Round   page 73
18. What's That Smell?   page 78
19. Ha Ha Halloween!   page 83
20. Thankful for Thanksgiving   page 89
21. Color You-Color Me   page 94
22. Inside the Nutcracker   page 99
23. Learning Curve   page 104
24. Oh Christmas Tree,   page 109
25. I Solemnly Resolve   page 114
26. On the Way to a Quilt Show   page 119

27. To Show or Not to Show	page 122
28. Judge Not	page 126
29. This Always Makes Me Laugh	page 129
30. On the Road to Hot Fudge	page 133
ANECDOTES	PAGES 137 to 141
The End	page 142

Chapter 1

First column for the Duluth News Tribune.

THE YEAR THE WORLD TOOK A TIME OUT

We let our hair go white, we hunkered down inside our homes, we learned to Zoom, we washed our hands a bazillion times a day, and we never touched our noses.

"What are we having for dinner?" became the most important question of the day and some of us delighted in trying new recipes, new ways of obtaining groceries, virtual family dinners, and some of us were reminded that we were never very good at cooking in the first place.

We made masks for ourselves and our loved ones, we made masks for our health-care workers, we wore masks, we forgot to wear our masks, and some railed against wearing masks, believing they had something to do with our civil liberties.

We chatted in our driveways, six feet apart and delivered things to each other's door knobs, quickly backing off like naughty Halloweeners. We didn't go to concerts, baseball games, or our children's school plays, because there weren't any. Some resourceful folks figured out ways to celebrate the graduating seniors not as they should have been, but as well as could be done.

Weddings were postponed, vacations were put off, 4th of July fireworks and parades cancelled. Thanksgiving and Christmas were spent in solitary every-day-ness or in risky gatherings that sometimes erupted two weeks later in group positives.

Violence escalated as people's anger grew against the unknown killer: the lost businesses and jobs; the hungry children; the rent; the car payment; the authorities. So many angry people with nothing to keep them occupied and feeling useful and productive.

Will the spiral ever reverse and start an upward climb? Maybe. Possibly. Hopefully. We've seen resourcefulness in figuring out alternative ways to do things and still be safe— church services and funeral memorials in parking lots, restaurants putting food trucks around town, a huge upswing in delivery services, companies that make liquor and automobiles also making disinfectant and respirators. An amazing list of ideas come to life. I mentioned resourcefulness. Ingenuity.

Determination. Positive thinking. Acceptance and compromise. Patience. With some kindness and thoughtfulness thrown in. I know, I know-- Pollyanna, Little Mary Sunshine, but giving up is not an option.

Come on 2021, heal us with your hope! Hit the road, 2020! May you diminish into just a nightmare in the history books.

And so, we wish for you all a healthy, Happy New Year. Look ahead. Don't look back!

Chapter 2

THE STUBBORN GARDENER

It's January in Northern Minnesota and the thermometer says nine degrees. There's white stuff all over out there, but I KNOW Spring is coming soon because I have been buried under a dozen nursery catalogues. The same ones come every Tuesday, as if I'm going to use them up before the next week. But yes, I have placed my orders. It's just such a "Long-Winter's-Eve-in-Minnesota" thing to do.

Fifty years ago, we came to Duluth and bought the Victorian house in Woodland, built on solid clay. I kept trying to grow things in the clay and wondering why I was such a rotten gardener. AFTER ALL--I came from "gardening people". My Mom and Dad had a huge garden in Upstate New York with grapevines and peach trees and Japanese Beetles. I earned a penny for each beetle I knocked off the grapevines into my little gasoline can. We lived next to a dairy farm and I remember my dad leaning out the attic window and shooting the barn rats off our corn stalks. BOOM! Well, it was only a .22, so it didn't really go BOOM! But to a little kid, it was pretty exciting.

In Duluth, with its 40 below Winters, we grow our roses with "The Minnesota Tip." Sounds like a Nordic drinking game, right? But, when the weather looks blustery, we rush outside armed with our garden spades. Behind each rose bush, we dig a little burial plot. Sticking the spade in front of the shivering little shrub, we TIP! Backwards into the trench it goes! Cover it up with dirt, pat it down-you can hear the little sigh as it dozes off. The hard part is remembering where you buried them, come Spring.

My biggest success in the clay garden was the Northern Lights azalea that grew to well over 7 feet tall. People would drive by just to see it in bloom and I felt like the greenest thumb ever, until I saw the original house plans. I had accidentally planted it over the old septic tank! That shrub was so happy you could hear it humming three streets over.

Then came the sandbox garden, next to an old gravel pit--in the middle of twenty acres of woods, where we built our great adventure--The Log House. I learned to *waterwaterwater* and *mulchmulchmulch*! And there were also Wild Animals. In the city, we had a few skunks under the front porch. In the woods, they popped up more often. One year, we bought a dozen bags of delicious-smelling cocoa bean mulch and laid them out on the driveway. Next morning, they were GONE! Not-A-Bean! AHA! DRAG MARKS! We followed the trails into the woods, where we found every single bag! All night long, each bag had been hauled away by a very industrious bear, chewed open, tasted and rejected. YUK!

Back to the City. Our "Prairie Rambler" is built on a granite ledge--as is most of Duluth. The first fall I tried to plant my 50 daffodil bulbs I had gotten from the catalogue, stuck my shovel into the dirt, and it went *CLUNK*! The granite was about 4 inches below the surface and in between were --- Buckthorn roots! Everywhere. Ab-so-lute-ly Un-garden-able! I spent the Winter trying to solve the problem. You would be shocked at how expensive 24 truckloads of dirt can be. THEN, I noticed galvanized containers-- square wash tubs, big round ones and HORSE TROUGHS! Pretty soon, three horse troughs showed up in my driveway. By this time the UPS guy knows that "the new people" are nuts anyway, so he doesn't even blink. He's delivered stranger things since they moved in--what's a few horse troughs? My obliging husband pounded drain holes and dragged the 46 tubs up into my "Tin Can Garden". Question-what will make it through the winter in a metal tub covered with bags of leaves and wrapped in aluminum insulation? Come Spring the answer was-two columbines and a delphinium.

I tried bargain annuals and summer bulbs. They barely started before the memorable wind storm came, blowing down one enormous pine that smooshed my tubs. Then came the Wettest Spring Ever. My dahlias grew to over 6 feet and bloomed like a technicolor movie. The Delphiniums were bodacious! The roses tried to hit the top of the 6-foot fence. My Tin Can Garden might work, after all.

    Next year, one can only hope. But, in January in Northern Minnesota, hope comes in the mailbox every Tuesday.

Chapter 3

RIVER'S BEND

Have you ever lived in a really old house? If not, then you have never been jolted awake in the night, wondering what that "funny" noise was. Could be some small fixable thing or it could be one of those biggies that translates to "Hello, Mr. Banker, I'm going to need a 2nd mortgage."

From the moment we drove up the scattered cinder driveway and stepped onto the sagging front steps, I knew we were supposed to live in that Old House. I didn't even hear the real estate agent say, "I know this isn't what you were looking for, *BUT*..." I did hear my husband, Tom, let out a loud groan. True enough, we were going to be SENSIBLE home buyers. We agreed- a small move-in-ready rambler, save up some money, get our bearings in a new city, blah, blah, blah. Then look for an old house. But there it was- Our Old House--for sale.

Tom said, "Well, I guess we could make them a low-ball offer." He was pretty convinced that the sellers would fall over laughing. He forgot that those same sellers had moved to another state; the house had been empty and on the market for seven months, the neighborhood kids were sure it was "haunted." It needed a new roof, the shingles were molting, the furnace was older than both of us—and worst of all—the beautiful quarter-sawn oak woodwork had been painted salmon pink. What was he thinking?! OF COURSE they accepted!

We were two adults, one just out of a Dermatology residency, three very small children, and a dog...maybe there was a guinea pig. We owned one rug, one brown corduroy couch, 4 box springs and mattresses plus a white Formica table and six black vinyl chairs, a sewing machine, and 43 boxes of books. And of course, some Power Rangers, Legos, a tricycle, and a couple of baby dolls.

Here we come, moving into an 1895 Queen Anne Victorian with a nameplate by the front door-"River's Bend." It had a formal parlor, a library, huge dining room, with a granite fireplace, a circular foyer with a Quezal chandelier and a grand entrance staircase. Our six-year-old quickly toured around the house, dog right behind him, and said, "Moooom, this is not a house. This is half a castle!!"

The first project- eliminating the pink paint. Armed with many gallons of stinky Zip-Strip and much determination, we waded in. EIGHT years later, we just couldn't do it anymore. We were starting to break out in hives just watching the Zip Strip ads on television. Our kids were whining about the ladders, cans of toxic chemicals, and box fans between their bedrooms and the bathroom. We painted the rest of the woodwork Chinese red. We rationalized that it went with the foyer wallpaper, which featured life-sized cavorting and gavotting people in Renaissance-era costumes. My motto became "Done is Good."

We always suspected there had to be a secret room in the house and my kids spent a lot of time and thought on that idea. They were sure it had to be under the big boxed-in landing for the grand staircase. That kept them busy for quite a while, and included an exploratory trip behind the built-in ovens. THEN, the boys discovered that removing the ceiling of the cupboard in their sister's bedroom, opened up A SPACE! A Secret Room, where they found-- HIDDEN TREASURE! A frowzy cardboard box holding comic books and school papers! And two empty liquor bottles! Proof that little boys had lived there before them.

I used to climb out onto the front porch roof to wash the windows. As our kids got older, they discovered that they too could go out their bedroom windows. Little sister had a balcony, middle son had the porch roof and oldest one the flat roof over the sunroom. They could come and go, evading their clueless parents who assumed they were in bed or doing homework. How silly were we?? One night, the oldest was just swinging down by his fingertips to land on the cellar door, before escaping into the neighborhood. As he was dangling in front of the kitchen window, I happened to be sitting across from it, having a late cup of coffee. We looked at each other through the window for a good ten seconds, then he slowly began to climb back up. STOMP, STOMP, STOMP!!! SLAM!! Busted!

River's Bend is a story to be continued. I hope you are nodding and smiling, remembering YOUR old house- or perhaps thanking your great good luck that you got out before the furnace gave its last wheeze.

Chapter 4

THE VISITORS

We lived at River's Bend for 21 years, a wonderful place for our kids to grow up. There was an enormous attic with old costumes to dress up in and old packing boxes for forts. It was the best place in the world for kids and friends to be, especially on a rainy summer's day. When the boys took up rock climbing, they would practice by going out the attic windows and rappelling down the side of the house, often leaving the windows open to the bats in the neighborhood.

Some of the most unusual visitors to "River's Bend" were the traveling puppeteers, before our time, in the 1940s and '50s. The attic had been turned into a theater with a 12-foot-high fly space where the performers could perch and dangle their characters in front of the wooden proscenium, telling their stories and entertaining the neighborhood. When they were finished, the resident artist would paint portraits of their star puppets on the walls up there. Very cool, but downright spooky.

Another attic project had to do with insulation—of which the thick walls and ceilings had none. Oh, maybe some old wadded-up newspaper here and there, but nothing serious. Tom and the boys rented a blower machine and hauled it and 28 bags of cellulose up the long flights of stairs. They took up the attic floorboards and got everything ready to blow insulation the next day. Pretty soon, a curious neighbor came by to see what we were up to, now. She climbed up stairs to the attic, just HAD to get a closer look and stepped onto the exposed plaster ceiling over the grand staircase. Screech!! There she went! All you could see from down below were her two legs dangling through the holes in the plaster, kicking like a threshing machine. Curiosity, cats, and all that.

    Our boys were showing a visiting buddy around the house, pointing out all the highlights including the laundry chute with a lift-up trap door at the end of the upstairs hallway. Nine year old boys love dares and this one resulted in a dive through the trap door and a plunge down three stories, around the sharp-angle turn half-way down, and into the waiting heap of dirty clothes at the bottom. I was in the kitchen, close to the downward pathway—Wowser!! I thought an eighteen-wheeler had veered off course and crashed into the back porch! "Hey, you guys, what's going on??!" "Oooohh nothing Mom, just playing with our trucks." Good thing I hadn't gotten to the laundry, that week!!

Back in the day, as our kids would say, going to school meant "walking to school." Our house was smack dab in the center of the three schools our children attended, grade school, Jr High, and High School. Washburn, Woodland, and East. So naturally, it was a gathering place for their friends, coming and going. Many times, I interrupted a kid's examination of the refrigerator contents only to have them turn out to be somebody I'd never seen before. "Hi. Who are you?" "Oh, hi, Mrs. Myers. Do you have any more milk?"

When you live in a house that has seen more than four generations, you have to think about the number of people who have tramped in and out over the years. River's Bend was 74 years old when we moved in, so realistically, there must have been at least 8 or 9 hundred people who had first-hand knowledge of the inside of our house. Which is a little creepy, when you think about it. SO many times, I would look out the kitchen window and see strange people wandering around the back yard. When confronted, they all had the same story--Their uncle Eustace or their cousin Edith used to live in our house and they have such fond memories of coming to visit -- did I think they could possibly----they had come all this way----"oh alllll right; come on in."

    One very elderly lady said that it seemed silly to her that we had eliminated the door between the parlor and the library. Why had we done that? Really??? If you looked at that wall, it was perfectly smooth, bumped right up against the fireplace--didn't hardly seem enough room for a door. But in 1983, when we built the kitchen addition, we needed to look at the original blueprints--and there it was!! THE DOOR! Right where she said it was.

Next chapter: how to build a new addition, with as much difficulty as possible.

Chapter 5

FIXING RIVER'S BEND

It all started as I was making dinner one sprinkly April evening and noticed that the peninsula electric stove-top had a big pool of water on top of it. Those darn kids! Where did that come from??! Then I noticed the plop plopping of large drops. This could not be good. Looking up, I was horrified to see the torrent of water pouring through the electric light fixture in the ceiling. Uh-oh, water/electricity= not good at all. We had replaced that flat roof once and patched it repeatedly. Time to get serious.

Since we were in a "historical" home, we thought it appropriate to contact an architect rather than just calling up Morty's Roofing and Repairs, and so we did. The young, enthusiastic architect showed up with his plans and his models and his overflowing briefcase of ideas. First, he showed us the sketch for a new roofing system on the old sunporch/kitchen area- Ho Hum. Then he showed us the detailed blueprints for that same area turned into a family room/kitchen area, but still under a flat roof. *Hmmmm.*

And THEN, he cleared off the table and set up his 3-D balsa-wood model of a breath-taking hexagonal gazebo-like structure that could only be built by ripping off the entire kitchen/sunroom/bathroom/back hall and back porch area. If you haven't guessed which one we went for, you haven't been paying attention. Of COURSE we did!! It had high ceilings and wood parquet floors. It had a porch with balusters and gingerbread trim. It had scalloped shingles and a grandiose, professional kitchen, with room for a beautiful table from the library. The final objection-killer was the little balcony overlooking it all from the opened-up second floor. The addition cost almost twice what we'd paid for the house. As our kids say, "Go big or go home."

We had never renovated a house before, never built a house before, never even put in a new bathroom sink. We were a little surprised when, just as the ink on the contract was drying, a driveway full of pick-up trucks, bulldozers and larger, unidentified grumbling mountains of machinery started pulling the back of the house off. Boom!! "Let's get er going, boys!!" You would think with a start like that, the project would be all finished the week after next, right?

Nope! Nine months later, we had the grand finale open house party. I could have had a baby. Thank God I didn't.

I believe the entire house being open to the world, the elements and the wildlife, surprised the contractor as well. He hadn't thought what to do while the footings, foundation, and concrete work was being done. I would lay in bed at night convinced I smelled skunk--that the skunks who lived under the front porch had moseyed in and were partying in the dining room.

Then there was the strange coincidence of the Old Jackson School being torn down, just when we needed all that interior woodwork. We spent two very cold days in that school, armed with crowbars and sawzall, filling up six small trailers with loads of quarter-sawn solid wood. Wainscoting, window frames and doors—Oooh the doors—8 foot tall solid oak doors with transom windows in 10 foot frames. Our teenage kids earned their spending money that summer by pulling nails and cleaning checkered wood. But the old wood was the perfect topper for the architect's plans. The Preservation Alliance approved. They gave us a plaque.

So now, our Victorian house was just the way we wanted it. As the years passed, the big old house vibrated with parties and celebrations, friends and visitors. We had joyous Christmases, birthdays and weddings. It was finally "The Myers House."

But then in 1990, the wallpaper with the Renaissance people was looking dated. The carpeting seemed scruffy and I knew I didn't want to redo it. I had done it the way I wanted, the first time. The children were grown and off on their own and I took up cross country skiing.

One snowy Sunday I came home from an exhilarating day on the Lester ski trail to find Tom grumbling over the upkeep bills on the old place. Eight months later, the scene opens to us and two large dogs living in a travel trailer in the middle of 20 acres of Northwoods. Over there, you could just see the shape of the big log house we were building. How did that happen? I'll tell you next chapter.

Chapter 6
FREEDOM TO READ

Do you love the heft of a hardcover book, so you can flip the pages back and forth, reading the good parts again? Or maybe the user-friendliness of a soft-cover paperback appeals, where you can jot down your notes or turn over page corners without fear of disciplinary action from the literary police?

Do you read with a Kindle? Does it have a "Kindleskin" stuck on the back, announcing your personality to all? And do you go into distress mode when you can't find it? Or forget to charge it? Yeah-all of the above; me too.

My mother actually taught me to read. You see, I attended kindergarten in Johnson City, New York, where half-day consisted of playing in the indoor sandbox, having juice, listening to the teacher reading, and naptime with your blankie. But no actual learning to read. My mom or dad read to me every night, but they were "big people." Of course they knew what the books said.

In September of that year, we moved to our new house in Vestal, NY. and I started 1st grade with Miss Kenyon. Not my biggest fan. She thought I was just a brat because I refused to read when she called on me. I started having "stomach aches" to keep from going to school, and sobbed at the bus stop every morning. So, Miss Kenyon summoned my mother to come in for a little talk and between the two of them, they figured out what was wrong. The children in my Vestal class had learned to read the year before, in kindergarten. When she called on me, I actually didn't know how to do what she was asking. And I spent the day being terrified that she was going to call on me. On the way home, my mother picked up a set of flashcards at the local drugstore and every night, we would drill. The other kids in my class had learned to read by rote- the "new-fangled" way. I learned phonetics and could always spell my way out of a paper bag, because of it. Thanks, Mom.

    My husband will proudly tell you that he learned to read with comic books. Tom's favorites were Plastic Man and Scrooge McDuck: an unlikely pair. All those Captain Marvel, Captain America, and Flyboy adventures paved the way to a reading habit that now favors Somerset Maugham and Ngaio Marsh. We have a standing family joke that if you mention any random subject at all, Tom will immediately jump to his feet and go to his library to find a book about it. We all look at each other, nodding our heads. "He's got a book about it." Yep, he even has a T-shirt that says so, right on the front.

    Between the ages of 8 and 12, I spent my entire summers reading. There was a sizable Weeping Willow tree in our front yard, and I would hide under its branches, my back up against the trunk, and read. I had my own card at our small "Free Library", about a mile from my house and once a week, I would take my stack of devoured books and walk down the road to swap for new ones, working my way down the aisles from fiction, to mysteries, to adventure and fairy tales., reading everything from Nancy Drew to Pearl Buck. It was Pearl Buck's "The Keys to the Kingdom" that got me into hot water with the staid librarian, who pursed up her lips and took it away from me, saying I was much too young to be reading trashy novels. I, of course, whined to my mom, who went storming down to the library all in a flap, me right behind her. "My daughter has our permission to read anything in this whole building. Don't EVER tell her she can't!" And she snatched the Pearl Buck off the counter and slammed out. Way to go, Mom!

Nowadays, I enjoy trying to figure out "who dun it" and mostly read murder mysteries: British cozies and brash young women private eyes, historical romantic intrigue, humorous bumbling detectives hiding their savvies beneath the put-on act. I am sad when a series comes to an end and delighted when I find a new writer with an impressive number of titles to read. I have noticed as I age, I no longer feel guilty about sitting down and reading a book in the middle of the afternoon; or staying up all night to finish a compelling story; or turning up the text size on my Kindle to "humongous" until I can see it.

Truthfully, I identify with Mrs. Pollifax, the 60-some grandmotherly lady in the flowered hat, who is actually a CIA agent, getting herself in and out of all sorts of terrifying scrapes. If I were 60 again, I'd get a big hat and apply to the Agency, myself. But I'm not, and never will be again, and for my part I am so grateful that Amazon always warns me that "you purchased this book in August of 2013" because I don't always remember. So much for the "attention to detail and steel trap memory" that CIA agents are supposed to have. At least I don't remember until I'm on page 47 and things start to sound familiar. "Oh Drat! I've read this one before!"

Chapter 7
GO BIG OR GET OUTTA HERE

When we bought the Victorian house, I fully intended, and said so on many occasions, to go out of that house feet first. I never planned on moving again. Ever. Ever. But in 1990, the kids were grown and on their own, I was coming to an end of my costume designing career and Tom was thinking about what he wanted to do after he retired from medicine. I had taken up cross-country skiing, not that I was any good at it, but it did get me out in the beautiful snowy woods, mostly standing at the top of a slight incline gathering my courage and making small, whimpery noises.

One snowy Sunday, shortly after Christmas, I came back from communing with the great outdoors, to find Tom grumbling about the upkeep bills on this great barn of a house. Usually when this happens, I find I have some pressing need to shut myself away in the bathroom but I was on a high--fresh air, trees, snow! So, THIS time I said--"Well, why don't we move, then?" Just like that--out of my mouth came words I never thought I'd hear!! I looked around to see who said that. And THEN I heard me say--"Let's build a log house." Who *WAS* this person who had taken over my body?

Well, Tom's ears perked right up and he pulled out a magazine--Log Home Living" and handed it to me with a great smirk on his face. "You mean like this?" And with that, we charged into what was to become one of the scariest adventures we ever, ever had.

When you decide to do something incredibly foolish, like build a log house when you've never even built a normal house, you dash out to Barnes and Noble and buy all the log home magazines they have. Next, you want to cut out all the pages with stuff you like and make a notebook. Very organized, yes? Then you gradually face reality, as you price how much all those fabulous things will cost you. Maybe you don't really need a glassed-in greenhouse off the front entryway, but you would like to keep the cement utility sink.

Second, look at all the possibilities-- peeled logs, milled logs, square logs, log siding on a frame house, cedar logs or dead-standing Lodgepole pine logs, Swedish cope, or chinked? Slanted corner cuts or straight? Dark brown stain, light grey, medium tan? Windows framed with log "bucks" or not. Log houses made from kiln-dried, yard-dried or green, wet logs with shrinkage pockets built in so the windows don't explode as the house shrinks and settles.

All this and you still don't have the property to put it on. AND you still don't have a bank. Banks are not happy about "unconventional buildings." They just say "NO! Uh-uh.." Sometimes they are sympathetic and say "I'm sorry, but not on your life!" A large log home was on page 2 in their handbook of unconventional buildings. Page one had to do with building on the side of a mountain in the Himalayas, with only a rope bridge to bring all the construction supplies to the site. But, since the financial stuff was Tom's domain, he got to trudge to all the banks, laying out his case about how trustworthy, responsible, mature, brave, reverent, and solvent we were.

Me, I was all about the design. My plan of action was this--I would narrow everything down to a few choices--- from the layout of the first floor to the water faucets in the powder room, and put it all out there so Tom could have a say, then pick what I wanted in the first place. I'm amazed we made it through with our marriage, sanity, and health intact. By all rights, Tom should have had an ulcer and I should have gradually curled into fetal position.

In Minnesota, large construction waits until the "load limits are off the road." By April, the frost was past, the ground would have "heaved," and the potholes would be smaller. I didn't say "be gone" did I? In Minnesota, they are never gone.

But things were looking up. Our realtor found a beautiful chunk of land. 20 acres of woods, swamp, and meadows and the first time we walked out on our new property on a cold, icy, March afternoon, we saw a snowy owl. And if that isn't a good omen, I'm turning in my know-it-all badge, right now.

Chapter 8

HOW TO DESIGN YOUR OWN LOG HOUSE

No, I am not, nor ever have been, a licensed architect. Yes, I didn't know what I was doing. But it made sense to me to use the measurements of the rooms we used in the Victorian house and plan the new house around the kitchen, where everybody always gathers. But not so fast; there are quirks and oddities about log houses.

A True Log House-- built with one layer of peeled logs that are visible inside and out, has an exterior log shell and interior wood-framed "boxes" for closets, bathrooms, and entries, like setting up toolsheds inside your house.

Log walls go up with no doors or window openings cut into them. They get chain-sawed out when the windows arrive. It's painful to watch "your" logs get big holes cut into them.

Log walls range from 12 to 18 inches thick and half that displacement comes out of your room size. Whoops! All of a sudden, you have to back into the powder room because there's not enough space to turn around.

Log houses are constructed at the log yard: first floor here, 2nd floor over there, roofing system beyond that. They are notched and stacked, numbered with little pieces of paper, disassembled, loaded onto semi-trucks and sent out over the road, to their building site, all in numerical order, where they are put up yet again, hopefully STILL in order.

Our log home company in Montrose, Colorado, had their own in-house architect who was capable of turning my doodles and scratches into actual blueprints that our builders could read. He came up with something called a "Valley Truss" for our roofing system. When you looked up, it was rather like being inside an upside-down "Tall Ship" A little disorienting, but fascinating.

The company always sent a supervising foreman to oversee the "putting up of the house" and work with the local contractors and carpenters. He was flying in on July 22 and the first of the log trucks was expected the next day. The other thing expected was our first grandchild--any minute, now. We arrived at the airport and waited patiently for the boss to appear. A voice close-by said "are you the

Myers's?" We turned to find a chunky teenage boy. "Hi, I'll be putting your house up." We must have looked like we were in shock, because he said "It's okey! My dad owns the company and I've been building log houses since I was just a kid." Ha! Must have been day-before-yesterday. Then he said he'd only be able to stay for two of the three-day build because he had to get back to Montrose. The State Rodeo competition was next weekend and he was on his high school rodeo clown team. We were still standing there with our mouths open. Teenage boy, log house, rodeo clown--nothing was computing.

    The only luggage he'd brought was his big tool bag, including his 28 pound sledge hammer. In the baggage claim, Tom said, "here, let me take that for you." It was like the cartoon skit where the box is nailed to the floor and the unsuspecting audience member tries to pick it up- Aaaahhhgggooofff! NOT budging!! The young man says, "nah, that's okey," and swung it up over his shoulder and off he went. We took him out for a steak dinner and then to the hospital, to introduce him to our new grandson, born that morning. After all, how many rodeo clowns do you get to meet on your very first day in the world?

The next morning, the big Peterbilt truck came rumbling up the dirt road, loaded with the first floor logs. You could see all the little paper numbers still attached. The huge rented crane started picking up the logs number by number and setting them down in their place, like Lincoln Logs. The carpenters were very cautious, wearing harnesses as they climbed up to nail the logs together. Next day, here came the second truck, with logs for the second floor. The local guys were starting to climb on top of the logs, but still hanging on. Third day, two trucks-the roofing system and the window "bucks." The guys were all up on the 2nd floor walls, 28 feet in the air, leaping from log to log, tool belts flying, pounding the huge iron stakes into the logs that would hold everything together. By the end of the 3rd day the house was "up."

Sometime in there, the audience arrived. Our kids came with lawn chairs, "liquid refreshments" and barbecue provisions, to cheer on the great adventure. But (cue the shark music) a new wave of crises was about to knock on the door. Next chapter.

Chapter 9

LOG HOUSE ADVENTURE RUN AMOK

You know how, when you start a challenging project there's a time of euphoria, when you handle all the "glitches" with determination and brilliant solutions and stiff-upper-lipness? Well, it was August 1st. The log house was up but nowhere near finished. The Victorian house had been sold, new people moving in on the 15th. 21 years of stuff had been packed up or gotten rid of. We had made a brand new quarter mile road to the new house, had a well drilled, and a septic dug. Oh, and the long-lost relatives we hadn't seen for maybe 46 years, had decided this was the perfect time to come and stay with us for a few days or more--- just before we moved out to our little temporary house which was meant to see us and our big dog, MacDuff through the building process, until the log house was finished. The relatives were still with us when the front doorbell rang and the young man standing there said "I'm really sorry but you know that house you were going to rent while your new one is being built? Well, I just sold it this morning...." Oh Boy! Where are those Tums?!

"Oh" he said, "and you wouldn't happen to want another dog, would you? I have to get rid of mine. She's just not working out. If you want to see her, she's tied to a tree in my front yard." WHAT?! Tied to a tree? My daughter and I jumped into the car to go and see this unfortunate dog. We drove back and forth in front of the man's house several times-no dog. Maybe someone else came and got her first. Oh wait, what is that fluff of hair you can just see by that poplar tree? Ohmigosh it's a blonde dog in a hole, chained to a tree, Oh poor thing, isn't she sweet?

That's how we wound up unexpectedly living "on site", in the middle of 20 acres of woods, sharing a 28 foot travel trailer with two large dogs: Rosie and MacDuff. Everything we owned was in storage and over there; you could see the log house coming along. We rationalized that it was a good thing for us to be available, in case the building crew had questions or problems. I became the "SHE" of "SHE SAID."

One afternoon we were in the camper, talking to the owner of the stone masonry company about the three-story TRIANGULAR-shaped chimney and fireplace we had chosen to build, and the insert that they were being built around, waiting in its packing case in the garage. Suddenly, there was a huge explosion of noise--like maybe the house fell down. We rushed outside, just in time to see the dust settling where the guys had cut out a big wide RECTANGLE of logs for the fireplace. "Uh guys…"

Another morning, we could hear MacDuff barking. Couldn't find him, anywhere. There he was---joyously wagging his tail, head poking out of the closest window in the log house-leaving his footprints where the guys had just poured the gypcrete for the in-floor heating. They are still there, under the tile floor.

One lovely Sunday afternoon a very long truck rolled up with a load of pale grey stone for the fireplace. The driver had brought his wife and made it a Sunday outing drive from Southern Wisconsin. He explained how he made a very good living, trucking grey rocks north, picking up colored river rock from our area, and driving it south. He said "Nobody's happy with what they've got, but it works for me."

For four months, while the crew banged and pounded. we lived in the trailer with the two big dogs. I made four bridesmaids dresses and one Mother-of-the-Bride outfit, all at the tiny kitchen table in the camper, using my little old Featherweight sewing machine. Mid-November came, and the trailer water and sewage systems were freezing up. Not good. The log house had no kitchen, no bathroom and no running water, no heat, no furniture. "The guys" put in one toilet and the basement utility sink. I cooked our meals with a hot plate and a microwave. We camped out through most of the winter. I don't even remember if we celebrated Christmas that year.

We lived in and loved that log house for 23 years. First there was the "5-Year Finishing Plan" which morphed into the "Ten-Year-Finishing Plan". There was a design glitch in the second story to be dealt with. Some huge roof logs were blocking the "would-be" entrance to the only guest bedroom up there. For about a year, until we figured it out, we had a guest room that happened to be inaccessible. So, of course, we named it "The Secret Bedroom." We snowshoed and gardened, cut trails, and saw bears, wolves, and moose.

One of the funniest things that used to happen were the phone calls from the home improvement guys. "Yeah, hey, we're having a big sale on our top-of-the-line aluminum siding. Can I come out and give you an estimate?" Big pause. Me: "I live in a log house." Silence. But you could hear the gears grinding as the pictures ran through his head...aluminum siding...log house. "Yeah, okey then. Bye."

Many milestones passed in that "unconventional building." Grandchildren were born, friends and relatives visited, weddings, Christmases, and birthdays were celebrated. In 2013, Tom and I were amazed to find that we had been married for 52 years. It was getting harder to mow those far meadows and the drive to and from downtown seemed longer and longer. Time to move back to town, leaving a chunk of our lives back on our trails. What a great time! Those thick, log walls must still ring with laughter---and some tears.

Next chapter, I'll tell you about some wild fishing trips, in honor of "the Minnesota Opener."

Chapter 10

HERE FISHIE, FISHIE

Northern Minnesota, Land of 10,000 Lakes and 43 trillion fish. Here, people fish for muskies and northerns, largemouth bass, walleyes, and crappies. Many people own a lake place. They call the lake places "cabins." At the tip of Lake Superior in Duluth, people fish off the ship canal for "lakers" in the summer, and drag their ice houses right out onto Lake Superior in the winter. They drill holes in the ice and settle down to stay warm and maybe catch a fish dinner. I LOVE to fish; but, not at 20 below. I can sit on an overturned bucket and drink beer in my garage. And, there's a bathroom much closer by.

I was born and raised in upstate New York, land of the Finger Lakes, where people fish for pickerel, perch, and pumpkinseeds. They have lake places that they call "cottages" or "camps" on lakes with names like Keuka, Skaneatlas, and Tuscarora. I started fishing with my mom and dad when I was very little. We would rent a small cottage on one of the closer lakes and spend our week fishing. My dad would row the three of us out to the middle of the lake, where they would sit all day with their lines in the water and I would play with my paper dolls. We *said* we were fishing.

Opening fishing weekend has always been a big deal with us starting when I was about four; we would head over to the Catskill Mountains to fish the small river that ran through the dairy farm of some friends in West Bovina, N.Y. Dairy/bovine? Nope, I didn't make that up. My mom would pack everything into our 1936 Ford and we would pick my dad up from work at exactly 5:00 and drive into the night, heading about 5 hours to the east. On this big dairy farm, just before "opening fishing" came "sugaring off," when they would tap the maple trees. We would stumble into that sleepy old farmhouse after the long drive, and the first thing that washed over you was the warm smell of maple sugar cakes, drying in the oven.

Sometimes, there were new baby calves to see. And there were always the huge draft horses you could catch a ride on. When you were a little kid, your feet stuck out on either side of their broad backs, like riding on an overstuffed couch.

We have a picture of my mother down by the river, wearing her favorite fishing outfit: a white blouse and a pair of riding jodhpurs. I have no idea where she got them; she wasn't a horse person. But she was standing there, holding at arm's length, the nasty-looking eel she had just caught and from the look on her face, you knew she was building up to a piercing scream.

Fondly remembering our childhood fishing vacations, Tom and I planned a few family adventures of our own. Day trips fishing on the Whiteface, weeks at the family cabin, and a houseboat trip into the Boundary Waters with three kids and a dog, to see the moose and the bears. The wildest animals we saw all week were chipmunks. And they had to be coaxed out of hiding with peanut butter.

When our kids were still little, we flew in on a big old rumble-y Beaver prop pontoon plane to a Canadian fishing camp, a place 25 miles and 7 portages away from the nearest scrap of humanity. "Oh please don't let anyone have an appendicitis attack" I mumbled, as we stood on the shoreline and watched the plane get smaller and smaller in the sky.

Once the kids got over the scary nighttime visits to the outhouse it was a wonderful time, fishing and swimming in the pristine wilderness and cool, quiet lake.

Just at dusk one day the guys were out fishing in the boat and middle son snagged into something that didn't budge. He and his little Zebco fishing rod tried their hardest, but finally, the immoveable object loomed out of the water, gave them all the fishy "stink eye" and plunged to the bottom of the lake, taking the Zebco (but not the kid) with it. Whoa! "Hey Dad, let's go back to the cabin and play Battleships, okey?" No late-night skinny-dipping THAT night!

So what do the kids remember about this wild adventure? That by the last morning, we had run out of milk and I made them put root beer on their Cheerios. You'd think they'd get over it, but *noooo*.

Chapter 11

MORE FISH TAILS

My husband is a very scientific fisherman. He reads everything he can about catching fish. When we go fishing, he's in charge of the location, the lures, trolling, or casting or jigging on the bottom. He always thinks if he hasn't gotten a hit in the first 15 minutes, the fish aren't there and we need to move on. I am in the other end of the boat. I am in charge of the anchor. I just get my line in and I hear--"Well, there's nothing here, let's move on." I reel in my line and pull up the anchor. Get to the next place, put the anchor down-- get the line in the water-- "Well, there's nothing here....pull up the anchor, wouldja?" My question--Is there a medal being given for "Superior Anchor Management With Temper Control"? Because I think I qualify.

Opening fishing weekend usually found us in a boat on a northern Minnesota lake, with some good friends. One year, the trip started out like a runaway train wreck and got worse from there. For the first thing, our friend hadn't fastened the latch on the boat hitch and when he stopped at the red light in the first little town up the Northshore, the boat--a very large boat--slammed into the back of his shiny new SUV, putting a lovely, big puncture wound through the trunk. Dang! Was he ever mad!

After a long, silent drive, we found that our rental cabin had been rented to someone else. Finally, we found a ratty place, and convinced ourselves that the strange smell coming from the crawl space didn't matter. But boy! Were we hungry! "Let's call it a day and have our opening night steak dinner." Well, our friend discovered that back home, when he'd re-arranged the fishing gear to fit in just one more tackle box, he forgot to put some things back into the boat--like all of the food except the bag with the mustard, ketchup, pancake syrup, and toilet paper. Long, silent trip back to town for dinner that night.

So the next day we'd better get out there and catch some fish; right? The first trip out, I kept hanging up on weeds and everybody would reel in while we poled over to untangle my lure. Then, we'd go back to where we were and toss our lines back in. And it would happen again. After about four times, Tom noticed I was just sitting there, looking at the scenery. I was stuck again, but didn't want to tell anyone. He quietly reached over and cut my line.

Because I clearly wasn't fishing, I was in charge of driving the boat. The fisher-people would point and I'd do my best to get us there, only one time I cut a sharp angle and the steering lever got stuck. We started spinning around in circles, with everybody's lines still out. First, I couldn't stop it because it was jammed. Then I couldn't stop it because we were all laughing so hard. Well, except Tom, who had gone out on the covered bow. We were going around and around, gaining speed, and he could only hold his rod straight up, hang on and yell. "Yow! Owww! Yeee-owww! Wow!" Like I said, bona fide train wreck. We cut it short and went home.

    Our one and only first and last canoe trip could have qualified for my story about "Disasters I Have Known." Here we were, coming DOWN the Kawishawi River on the last day of our first canoe adventure, and the howling 50 mile per hour winds were going UP. It had rained every day for five days and not a single fish dinner had crossed our lips. We were with another couple- he being a wilderness guide and she a former camp counselor- both very experienced campers. By this time, I believe they had had a little spat and she was spending most of her time in the tent, reading paperbacks. No singing around the campfire for us! Tom was still gimping around in his burned-up boot that I had tried to dry out by the campfire and our sleeping bags were very soggy. It wasn't looking good to make it to base camp that night, so the hot showers and grilled steaks were probably going to be a "not happening." With no campsites nearby and darkness coming on, we put up our tents on the first chunk of solid rock we found. I remember going to sleep, wondering if that very tall red pine above us would come crashing down in the night. The next morning- a miracle happened. The sun came out and we could go HOME. The canoe trip was DONE. And we didn't EVER have to do it again!

Chapter 12

NEW AND IMPROVED

Many companies periodically make changes in their products and announce that they are "New and Improved." Usually that means that the former product which you searched for forever and loved, relied on, recommended to friends, and can't live without, will no longer be available. Except in its "new and improved" state. Which is to say, "not available."

I have an electric egg poacher that was given to me as a bridal shower gift 60 years ago and is still working away. Evidently, it never needed improving, because the company is still making similar ones and people are still buying them. I always joked that when the egg poacher quits working, the marriage is over. Good for a laugh, until it got close to six decades. Now, I'm starting to get a little nervous. What happens if it does stop working? Will I have to buy a "new and improved" one? Or will there be a "new and improved" me?

To me, "improved" usually means something needed improving. I always wonder if the improvers succeeded in their improvements.

I once had a Dodge Durango. I loved that car. It was the perfect size for me to drive, and had the perfect cargo space for costumes, antique furniture, dogs, whatever. I drove it for years. Then it started showing its age-making mysterious crackly noises, and sucking up too much oil. Time to trade it in. But the Durango people had "improved" upon my car. It was now heavier by a ton or two, the size was approaching that of a Mack truck, and $$$ zoomed to $$$$$. Improvements? Hardly!

 I don't know what the literary policy is about mentioning "unmentionables" but let's talk underwear- specifically bottoms, both sexes. For years, you've searched for The Perfect Underwear. You've gone through the high cut, low cut, stretchy polyester, Scottie dogs, and sports teams briefs until Oh Happy Day! you find The Ones. They bend when you do, don't sag where you don't, don't ride up, don't fall down, and they don't lose themselves in your washing machine. They come in four solid colors, all your favorites—and camo. You rush out to buy some more of those babies- right now! But, so sorry; you can't. Nope; really you can't. They've been discontinued by the manufacturer. One of their analysts did a study. The pre-production cost estimates were miscalculated and the company is losing 37 cents on every pair you buy. Too bad; so sad.

My husband has a gasoline-driven garden wagon. He's had it for about 25 years, has taken very good care of it, and it works just fine. Last year, the tires were flat and looked like they were split, so he contacted the company to order new tires. Uh-oh. They no longer stock those tires. But, do they still make that model garden wagon? "Yes, yes, we do. But it's been improved." Husband: "What do you do for tires?" Company: "Different size, different tire, won't work for your wagon." Husband: "What's the solution?" Company: "Uh…... new wagon?" Husband: "No Way."

Back to the subject of wedding gifts that didn't need improving: where are those wonderful sheets and pillowcases that we got in the 50s and 60s? They weren't silky and sleazy; they were crisp. They didn't wrap themselves around your neck, and they DIDN'T HAVE TO BE IRONED!! Yes, I know they weren't pure 100% organic cotton and they had polyester in them, and maybe they "pilled" after a while, but they DIDN'T HAVE TO BE IRONED! Now, you get "wrinkle-free" sheets that come out of the dryer looking like dried-up tumbleweeds.

Toasters were another popular wedding gift, 60 years ago. Sometimes you got 3 or 4. They amazingly toasted all four corners of your bread, on both sides. In 60 years, I've probably owned 18 toasters. The one I have now is two years old and only toasts the bread on the top half. I've gotten used to turning the bread around, half-way through. You have to learn to deal with these "improvements."

In the early 1960s, all brides got a set of metal ECCO kitchen utensils. They had matching plastic handles printed with an attractive Pennsylvania Dutch design and included a hanging rack. The set consisted of a spatula, cake server, sieve, slotted spoon, solid spoon, and an egg beater. The solid spoon found its way to the kids' sandbox; the spatula and the egg beater lost their handles, and the rest gradually wandered off.

But I still have the slotted spoon. I would have to say that this product has been improved. They are now made entirely of plastic or nylon. And I would be willing to bet my egg poacher they will make it through 60 years, handles and all. So, 60 years of marriage and I still have the original egg poacher, slotted spoon, and husband. No improvements needed, thank you very much.

Chapter 13

Disasters I Have Known

I've always felt that I have led a pretty great life. Most of the good things have come about because I was in the right place at the right time. I met my husband because I was working in the flower shop when he came in to buy flowers for his date that night. That was a good thing---right??

However, just like everyone, I've had those "End of the World" catastrophes when the only thing that will make it better is a "do-over." They sound like this:

"OMG, OMG, OMG!" DEEP BREATH, SIT DOWN---and THINK! How can I fix this?

Disasters are a relative thing. They come in all sizes. There is the bad-hair-zit-on-your-nose-while–having-your-Senior-picture-taken type of disaster. At the time, this might seem monumental but in the grand scheme of things, it probably isn't. Then, there's the "new neighbors across the street coming for dinner, when you've just burnt up the main course" type of disaster. This takes a little creative thinking, but you can deal with it. There's a can of Spam and some cooking sherry in the pantry.

Then, there are those pretty spectacular disasters that involve significant injury and broken parts. One of mine had to do with being at the top of an 8-foot stepladder hanging onto a Dirt Devil vacuum cleaner, sucking up the sawdust from the new shelving in our renovated kitchen....and falling on my back with said vacuum cleaner coming two seconds later. My husband, being a physician, said the same thing he always says: "you're okey. I'm sure it's just a sprain," resulting in a few hours spent with a bag of frozen peas on the part that hurts, until making the inevitable trip to the ER.

Usually, those kinds of disasters can be chalked up to: (#1) stairs or ladders; (#2) armloads of things; (#3) moving backwards. Yessss- I know. "Stupid!! That was really Stupid!!" I am currently banned from ladders.

Then, there are the "memory lapse" type of disasters. You drove all the way home, 10 miles out in the country but forgot to load up your groceries at the supermarket, way back in town. Again. It's even worse when it involves waiting children.

Here's a "faux pas" disaster. You make a big to-do about your son-in-law's birthday- delivering a nicely wrapped present, a hardware store gift certificate, and a sappy birthday card, only to have your daughter text you with this message--"Motherrrr his birthday is NEXT month." Dang!

My husband is very serious about having everything packed just right for a road-trip, leaving within 4 minutes of our specified leaving time, arriving when we said, all that grown-up stuff. So here we are, all in the car, driving south on Hwy 35, kids in the back, fighting over who gets the peanut M&Ms and who gets the plain ones. It's a VERY hot summer day. We're all in shorts and minimal clothing, on our way to Tom's sister's wedding. We're both attendants. It's a pretty formal, big church ceremony and country club reception, all that whoop-de-do.

We got a late start because the dog was hiding and had to go to the kennel. BUT we're making good time now, and we should get there with minutes to spare before we have to change clothes and head to the church. Clothes?? What clothes? I think we took the clothes out of the car to take the dog to the kennel. I have the long dress I'm wearing for the ceremony, plastic-wrapped, no shoes. The kids are okey; they're young enough to be summer-scruffy. Tom is in gym shorts and sneakers- no long pants, no shirt, no tie. His sister's wedding. Church. Country Club. DISASTER!

OMG,OMG,OMG. DEEP BREATH, SIT DOWN, THINK! Where's the closest men's wear shop? I'll drive, keep the motor running, you run in, grab the first pair of grey slacks. Try to not make it the $300 pair…maybe a shirt, too? Forget the tie! Let's go!

AND then there's my favorite- going to the drive-through car wash, you accidently leave your cross-country skis strapped to the top of your car. You leap out half-way through the wash cycle to try and rescue your skis from the soapy octopus that's trying to gobble them up. Arriving home, dripping suds, carrying 1 and 1/2 skis, sporting the beginning of a black eye, you find your spouse waiting. "The Scrub and Dub called. They're closed until the parts come in for their broken car wash machine. They'd like you to stop in and have a little chat with the manager."

Chapter 14

Whaddya Say Where You Come From?

My friend from Baltimore that used to come out and visit every August and December loved to make fun of our Minnesota accent. He would say, with a cheeky grin and a loud voice "oh fer shure you got some cyuute shews, dere."

I, being born and raised in Upstate New York, was positive that I had no such thing as a funny accent. When I came to Minnesota in 1957, I might have been wearing "sneakers." But after time had passed, I was wearing "tennis shoes." I suppose after 65 years, I might have picked up a tiny bit of a Minnesota sound. Dontcha know.

I once got a big laugh from a California crowd at a quilt retreat by saying "Hi dere, Yaaa hey, I'm here from Minnnnah-SUO-tah!" Then I had a hard time convincing them that we really don't actually talk like that. Do we? Of course, they had all seen the movie "Fargo" so they weren't going to listen to me. They'd heard it with their own ears.

I have a friend who always says when I show her one of my completed quilts, "Aww, didn't that come nice?!" Plus, she usually hands me a delicious-smelling bag and says "I brought you some bakery", rather than "cookies or bars." Speaking of food, when my parents and I moved to Minnesota from N.Y., we couldn't find any "Hot Pie," meaning pizza. We would be directed to the nearest bakery for apple or blueberry. In New York you can also score some pizza by just asking for a "slice." But, you can't get anything to drink by ordering "pop" as you would here. You have to order "soda" or "soft drink." Then you get your "purse" out of your "pock-a-book" to pay for it. If you're in Minnesota you would probably say, "let me get my *beg*." If you're south of Illinois you would say, "Ah'll git mah bay-- -ugg"- two syllables. And you probably ordered a "Co-cola", anyway.

Now, please don't get me wrong. I'm not making fun of the way anybody speaks or the phrases they use. I find it all pretty fascinating, don't you? Where did these phrases come from?

We had some neighbors in Rochester, Minnesota. They were originally from Waterloo,

Iowa, and when describing something that took a long time, Betty would say, "It took 'til Who Laid the Rail." What the heck does that mean? Do you know who is Who?" And where did he put his rail? And what took him so long? Now I sound like Abbott and Costello. Who's on First?

So being raised in New York, you would probably expect that I would have that New Yawker way of speaking, like Fran Drescher in the Television sitcom, "The Nanny." I remember reading that Fran took voice lessons, at great expense, to try and get rid of that accent and her snort of laughter. Like "pounding money down a rathole," it didn't do any good. That wise-cracking voice is the real Fran Drescher. However, being about 185 miles due northwest of Manhattan in the small town of Vestal, we just never picked up that east coast twang. We did say "ruff" instead of "roooof," and our front steps were called "stoops." And my mom always said "Aayuh" when she meant "yes".

But you also have "stoops" in Baltimore, where I used to go 2 or 3 times a year to work for the Opera. However, there they are white marble and get meticulously scrubbed if there's a conscientious housewife in residence- a point of pride. There I was called "Huun" by the friendly waitress who would ask "Whadda youse want, Huun?" The city was "Bwaula-mer" and in the summer everyone went "Danneeoshun" (down to the beach).

Some friends were driving to the big National quilt show in Kentucky one year and asked me if I wanted to "come with." We decided to take an impressive detour and go by Elvis' house in Memphis on the way. Along the highway, we kept seeing billboards for a restaurant that claimed to be "The Home of the Throwed Rolls." Finally, we couldn't stand it anymore and went at least 20 miles out of our way to check this out and learn exactly what was a "Throwed Roll." Anyhoo, we get to this place which is kind of an "all you can eat" establishment, and get settled into a table with built-in benches, sorta like grade school. We're lookin at the menu, thinkin it was "kinda spendy," when the waiter comes by and says the buffet is the best bet, so we order that. Before we could even mosey on over to the salad bar, this guy comes boomin out the kitchen door with a whoop and a holler, carrying a big dishpan and barbecue tongs. He reaches his tongs into the pan, pulls out a big butter roll and flings it at the guy at the table next to us, who leaps up and makes the catch, pretty as you please. All around us, folks clapped. Woohoo!

We three look at each other, the lightbulb comin' on over our heads, "Throwed Rolls" just like the billboard said. Mystery solved. Good thing, because the next ones came right at US. "Aw, Jeez Louise! Watch out you guys! Here they come!!"

Minnesota Accent? You talkin' to Me? Silly You. I don't have an accent. Whaddya talkin' about!

Chapter 15

PETS AND PETS AND PETS

I am, always was and always will be, an only child, born when my mom was 28. In those days, women had their children at a younger age, which meant that I was a "Late-in-life-only-child." Huuuuuge potential for being spoiled rotten, there! So, probably to compensate for my "alone-ness", we had lots of pets. I'm talking not only puppies and kitties. I'm talking lizards, hamsters, ducks, chameleons, bunnies, tadpoles, and CHICKENS!

In 1943, when I was very little, some well-meaning relative gave me three baby chicks for Easter- a pink one, a blue one, and a yellow one. The pink and blue ones had been colored with toxic dye and sadly, they quickly turned up their little toes. The yellow one was "au natural" and she grew into a real chicken named "Susie," who followed me everywhere. Susie wore the same size clothes as my dolly, "Sweetie Pie" and even had the same taste in baby bonnets. She would patiently let me dress her up and wheel her around the neighborhood in my doll buggy. We were an odd pair. One morning, however, Susie was missing. My Mom explained that Susie had grown tired of city life and had gone back to live on the farm. I often wondered just how she got there.

The town I grew up in was very small: 743 people in all, and boasted a little old Victorian train station. Our whole family was at the depot one Saturday afternoon, waving to my Uncle Claude as the train started to pull away, headed for Penn Yann, N.Y. Suddenly down the street, honking all the way, barreled this large tan duck, determined to make the train. Just as he dove under the wheels, my dad made a grab and got him by one foot. The duck was not happy about missing his train and really let him know it, hissing and snapping. The story later came out that a young farmhand had brought him into the local bar with hopes of trading him in for a few beers. When the duck pooped on the gleaming mahogany bar, as ducks will do, the bartender scooped him up and threw him out the front door. Nobody seemed to want him back, so the duck came home to live with us- in the basement, where he pooped and honked to his heart's content. My mother stood him for as long as she could but one morning I awoke to find that "Uncle Ducky" had joined Susie out at the farm. My mother said he took the bus.

Then there was The Hamster Family- plural and more plural. You would think that my two sensible adult parents would know better than to buy a little kid TWO hamsters: a boy hamster, Chucky; and a girl hamster, Doreen- a very chubby, fluffy little girl hamster. My dad built them a tiny cage- singular. Their new home. Next day there were six hamsters; little Doreen was evidently not just chubby but very pregnant. So, my dad knocked together more cages...and more. It has been said that it is very difficult to determine the sex of a hamster. They don't seem to have any problem at all.

The pet shop owner was very gracious and took our 23 hamsters in on trade towards a new puppy, and, 7 years old, I discovered DOGS. That puppy was Daisy Moppet, a fluffy white terrier type. Since then, there has been Mitzi, Heidi, and Tina, the dachshund trio who starred in my childhood doodles of their great adventures. There was Clancy from the Minneapolis animal shelter, named after my kids' TV hero of the time. Then came the Big Dogs- the English sheepdog/black lab/poodle mixes. There was MacDuff the Mighty, twins Toby and Dudley (don't ever go to get a puppy when there are only two left), Gus the Gorgeous, born in Twig, Rudy from Peavey, S.D., and now Jordie the wild one. Every morning, Rudy would come with that look… "is he leaving, yet?" And I can't forget Rosie O'Grady, the dog in the hole and the only dog I ever knew who would bark at a jet trail and convince you she could see it.

The middle son took custody of Rosie O'Grady when he was instrumental in making the decision that I should bring home not one sheepdog/lab puppy, but two- Toby and Dudley. Because, of course…well, I'm sure you've heard this argument before… Can't be responsible for a sad puppy, can we? Our son, who has the same last name as we do- Myers- took Rosie to the groomers and later got the call: "Mr. O'Grady? Yer dog's ready."

Good dogs; every one of them. No matter how flawed your personality, how cranky your day, how awful your hair looks or that you have a big pimple on your nose, your dog will look at you like you have just been awarded the Nobel Peace Prize. They are amazed by everything you do and can hardly wait to see what's next. If there is a shortcoming with dogs, it would be a design flaw that their Maker should have foreseen—a dog should last for a lifetime—your lifetime.

I'm sure with all the early pets, my parents meant to make me a kind, responsible, unspoiled child who would become a kind, responsible adult. Maybe it worked…maybe it didn't. I surely loved every pet I ever had, but I'm thinking the spoiled part was a lost cause.

In the next chapter I'll tell you how Toby saved me from the moose.

Chapter 16

IT'S ALL ABOUT THE DOGS

When I was growing up, we had a red standard dachshund named Mitzi. She loved the water and was just long enough in the body, with her little legs splayed out front and back, to balance on an inner tube, floating around whatever lake we were visiting. My mom couldn't swim, but she also enjoyed being in the water, so my dad always brought two inner tubes on vacation and my mom and Mitzi would blissfully float around, tied together. I was never sure which one was driving.

One year, our labradoodle Gus and I asked for a puppy for Christmas. Tom and I were still out on our 20 acres of woods and having friends over was easy for me, but not so much for Gus. He seemed lonely. So right after the holiday, through a white-out blizzard, Tom and I drove to Peavey, South Dakota, home of a retired dairy farmer-turned-doodle-breeder and picked out Rudy, the little blonde guy with the bent tail and the adorable "over-the-shoulder" look. He seemed the mellowest, least bossy pup in the litter, and we knew that would sit well with Gus, the "Alpha Dog." On the way home, we wrangled about names. Eugene (after my grandfather), Rowdy Doodle, and Howard were all rejected. We finally settled on Rudy, after the former governor of Minnesota. We felt that would give him something to live up to.

The thing about having one dog, is that they are YOUR dog. They hang with you; they are part of your clan. You do stuff together. With two dogs they form their own club, egg each other on, and take turns thinking up trouble. Gus had rarely ever left our large yard by himself but now with Rudy for a sidekick, out the door meant "into the woods." There were wolves in those woods. We tried tying them both up; they whined and barked. We tried tying one of them up. One whined, the other barked. Finally, Tom hit on the solution. He got about 15 feet of rope and tied them to each other. They never could agree where to go, so they didn't go anywhere.

Before Gus and Rudy, there was Toby. He was a big, lovable barn puppy and my companion after we moved into the north woods. I was intrigued with everything woodsy including making trails down to the river, identifying the wild plants, and animal scat. We had watched a local television show about a man setting up his tree stand and calling moose with a birchbark megaphone. Fascinating! I knew we had moose on our 20 acres because I had seen their "leavings."

So one snowy day, all on our own, Toby and I headed for the northern property line. I was on my snowshoes breaking trail, with Toby bringing up the rear. I'm standing there, about 15 acres away from my house, looking into the dense woods, and I let loose with a series of noises that I thought sounded like, "hey, big boy. Come over here and let me take your picture." Pretty good, I thought. Toby gave me the "What! Are you crazy?" look and headed back the way we had come, galloping all the way. I never thought Toby was a PHD but that day, he was the smart one on the team!

You have to admit, you gotta love puppies. Even when they think your new Italian loafers are the special dog chew toy you bought just for him. The first paycheck I ever earned bought a new puppy. But they take a lot of energy and can wear you out. Our current pup, Jordie, runs on two speeds: stop and go. The very minute he falls asleep, we both lay down to take a nice little nap, ourselves. Once, he woke up first, grabbed and ran away with my brand new eyeglasses, and chewed them to little bits and pieces. When I found the pitiful left-over clumps and took them into the optical shop to beg for help, they said, with a knowing smile, "oh, gotcherself a new pup, eh?"

Puppies also love hearing aids. Ask me how I know.

We have several long-standing Christmas traditions in our house. One is that Santa still fills stockings for my kids, even though they are well into adulthood. I always help out by gathering some treats, some reading material to keep everyone occupied before dinner, and always some funny items because I love to hear them laugh. Another tradition is that middle son, his wife, and his dog come for Christmas Eve and we go out for Chinese food.

The dog waits at home and reports on whether Santa has been there, yet. One year, we came home to find that Bailey, the 165 pound Newfie, just couldn't wait for Santa and got into my bag of treats and ate all the red wax lips that were the "ha-ha" part of the stocking stuffers. Just think about a big black Newfoundland wearing a guilty expression and red wax lips. Try not to laugh. I dare you.

RUDY IN THE GARDEN "THE STUBBORN GARDNER"

THE TIN CAN GARDEN "THE STUBBORN GARDNER"

"RIVER'S BEND", "VISITORS" and "FIXING RIVER'S BEND"

**"THE MID-LIFE CRISIS- BUILDING THE LOG HOUSE",
"DESIGNING YOUR OWN LOG HOUSE" AND
"LOG HOUSE RUNS AMOK"**

"HERE FISHIE, FISHIE"

GUS AND RUDY

JORDIE

BAILEY FROM "IT'S ALL ABOUT THE DOGS"

"HA HA HALLOWEEN"

"INSIDE THE NUTCRACKER"

"HA HA HALLOWEEN" AT A.T. JONES COSTUMERS

THE TOO TALL TREE

"OH, OH! CHRISTMAS TREE"

"WILT THE STILT TREE

THE ARTSY FARTSY QUILT, "HEARTTHROB"

"PASSIONFLOWER" FROM "TO SHOW OR NOT TO SHOW", MOST USE OF COLOR

Chapter 17

MUSIC MAKES THE FAMILY GO 'ROUND

As far as I'm aware, my family boasts no classical pianists nor opera Divas. I wouldn't say that we are particularly musical, unless you count the bagpipes as a musical instrument which some people refuse to do, considering their original purpose was to scare the bejeezus out of whichever warring clan the pipers were up against that week. I, however, love the pipes and drums and once spent an entire afternoon following the Winnipeg Police Pipe Band around Miller Hill Mall, until they started getting nervous and asked me to leave. We happen to count several quite accomplished pipers in our family group, including one who is pipe major and Founding Father to Twin Cities Metro Pipe Band. They wear the Clark tartan in honor of my father, the late Ray Clark who would probably be surprised to hear that, since he was Welsh. Along with practicing and performing original musical pieces in Midwest competitions and participating in parades, the fun-loving Metro band enjoys bedeviling their pipe major, like the road trip when they duct taped his motel room door completely shut, except for the peephole.

Apparently, the love of music does not eliminate love of mischief-making.

My father, mentioned above, did not play an instrument that I know of, but he loved to dance and he and my mother were very smooth movers in the big band days. My mother, being a Flapper-ish teenager in the 1920s, played the ukulele with some skill and taught me to play "My Little Grass Shack" when I was 6. At 8, she gave me a choice; I could take piano lessons or tap dancing lessons. I had to think about that one. I had two friends who were learning to play the piano. All I ever heard them do were the scales, up and down, up and down, do it again. And they talked about HAVING to practice like they dreaded it. Tap dancers, on the other hand, wore sparkly costumes, shoes that made a lot of noise and lipstick. Piano players did none of those things. Not a very hard decision, after all.

We little tappers had our Saturday morning lessons in the old gymnasium at the Elks' Club in downtown Endicott and in the afternoon, we would perform for the bar patrons, who thought we were adorable and gave us standing ovations. The added bonus was that my mother found her niche- sewing the fluffy little skirts and shiny headpieces that we strutted around in. From then on, our kitchen table always had a corner piled high with sequins and netting. Tap dancers, however, learn time steps and routines. Pianists learn to read music, which I didn't get to do. And I did love to sing. I sang in the Jr. High and high school choirs; I sang in school Gilbert and Sullivans; I sang in a girl's trio- "Three Little Maids From School Are We." Lalalalala. And I sang in the Presbyterian church choir, where I met my husband.

    He had opted for the piano lessons overseen by a very strict nun, who rapped him on the knuckles with a wooden ruler for a wrongly played note. When I met him, his repertoire included "Fur Elise" on the piano, some jolly tunes on his square box concertina, and several selections of twangy vibrational melodies on the mandolin. I was enthralled. I was dating a musician! In addition, he gave me my very first classical record, "Invitation to the Ball," setting me on the path of music appreciation that went beyond Bill Haley and "Rock Around the Clock." He (husband) had a fine tenor voice much admired in choral groups, those tenors. He was tapped to sing in his college glee club and traveled all over Europe one summer, singing for crowned heads and papal people. It was the experience of a lifetime and he still has stories to tell, about wearing paper collars and cuffs, sleeping in a Scottish haystack and flying in a converted DC-3 plane, sporting "May West" life preservers all the way across the ocean.

In the 1960s, while living in Germany, courtesy of the U.S Air Force, we bought a lovely, handmade German guitar and I took some lessons. I sang folk songs and learned how to "hammer on". "Pretty Peggy-O" and "The Silkie", sang I. I grew my hair very long and thought I was Joan Baez. But guess what? I wasn't even close.

As teenagers, our children tried their hands at saxophone, flute, banjo, violin, and mandolin. Our oldest started playing my guitar. When he quickly became more accomplished on my instrument than I ever was, I gave up my dreams of a lucrative recording career (big sigh), passed the guitar on, and cut my hair. Eventually, the guitar became the musical training wheels for our grandsons, suffering some dry winter splits and a buckled keyboard. But the story of the handmade German guitar has a fairytale ending. It was purchased by a man who restored its original beauty and sound. Even better, he did it with the help of the son of the original maker, whom he searched for and found, still making handmade guitars at the family business in Germany. Happy endings are the best, aren't they?

Chapter 18

WHAT'S THAT SMELL?

Your mother holds a milk bottle up to your nose and says, "Would you smell this and tell me if it's gone sour?" Eeeuwww.

The word "smell" is one of those that have several different meanings without altering their spelling. Well, huh! Your mother wants you to smell (verb) the milk for her because her sense of smell (adverb) tells her that there is a bad smell (noun) coming from the milk bottle.

One of the side effects of having the Covid virus seems to be losing your sense of smell. Not a good thing! "Tom, do I have on too much perfume? Is that why your eyes are watering?" And if your sense of smell is gone, suddenly you can't taste your favorite pizza or mashed potatoes and cream gravy. You'd think you'd lose a lot of weight, wouldn't you? That you'd become your old 29 year old self again? That you'd just eat crunchy vegetables and things that are good for you? Nope! Not going to happen! Always hoping I'll be able to taste that next thing.

Not only (and here's my point) does that loss wipe out your awareness of the world around you and your enjoyment of food and drink, but you lose the ability to conjure up all manner of memories, good and bad, that are triggered by certain scents.

When I say, "the aged wood smell of an old fishing cabin" do you know what I mean? Can you smell it? Every once in a while, I come across that distinctive odor and I not only see the good times at the family cabin, forty years ago, but the cottages we visited on the Finger Lakes in New York, when I was a child- oil lamps, kerosene stoves, and dried, unfinished interior wood walls.

On the opposite end, I was working at a florist in Minneapolis when I was pregnant with our first baby. They had moved me from the wedding department, where the floors are sometimes slimy with cut stems to dried flower bouquets, so I wouldn't fall down. The trouble came with the smell of the linoleum adhesive which was used to hold the Styrofoam bases in the flower bowls and vases. I just had to pass through the door to that department and I was off to the bathroom to lose my breakfast. Sorry to dwell on it, but that smell still has the power to turn me green.

The lilacs have just finished blooming as I write this. Most of us love the smell of lilacs and have fond memories of our grandmother's lilac hedges. Our lilacs are right up against the front of our house. When they first start to bloom, we open the windows to let in the glorious perfume. But two weeks later, we keep them tightly closed as the lilacs pass their prime and start to reek of dead flowers. It's enough to wake you out of a sound sleep. Oh boy!

Have you ever ridden in a sled behind a team of exuberant dogs as they explode onto the snowy trail? Whew! Explode is the operative word here, for what happens as the dogs take off. I had no idea.

And then, there are the good smells: cotton candy and mini doughnuts means the State Fair. Burgers on the grill smell means it's finally summer. The smell of bacon sizzling in a cast iron pan ties in with the old dried cabin wood walls. Estee Lauder was the perfume my wonderful mother-in-law wore. I smell it and there she is! New car smell. New carpeting smell. Puppy breath. Baby skin. Autumn leaves.

Dirt. I like the smell of dirt. Christmas trees and chocolate cake just out of the oven.

    Your sense of smell can even save your life. When we lived in our log house out in the woods, I would walk out to the main road to pick up the mail. On the way back one day, I could smell a musky odor, similar to skunk. I thought, "oh no, where is the dog? Did he follow me? Is he going to get sprayed? Do I have tomato juice on hand?" Then I looked up and there were a couple of baby bears up in the tree right beside the road. Right there! Holy Cow! Where is Mom? She must be around here, somewhere! They were good babies and stayed up there as I tried to mosey past without alarming anyone. Once past them, I tore down the road, rushed into the house and slammed the door! I sat there shaking on the boot bench and a funny thought occurred to me. I wondered if I smelled as bad to them as they did to me.

    I mentioned in a previous column that when I was just little, my family made a yearly trek to a dairy farm situated on a trout stream in the Catskill Mountains, for opening fishing weekend. Our farmer friend had always just finished tapping his maple trees when we got there and even after seventy-some years, pancake breakfasts have a mingled scent – warm maple syrup, old farmhouse, and cows.

If I can send you all a positive wish, here it is: "May all of your memories be smelly."

Chapter 19
HA, HA HALLOWEEN!

I don't get all worked up about Halloween, but I know people who do. I have friends in the theater world whose year-long project is how best to astound their friends and neighbors with their Halloween costume extravaganzas. They even send out postcards with pictures.

I got over that in sixth grade. My mother had made me a perfectly lovely witch costume, pointy hat and all, so I was excited to show it off at school. Halfway through the day, the kids who had brought costumes were allowed to go to the washroom and put them on. So, here I come in my spiffy witch outfit, thinking I looked really wicked and right behind me comes Irene, prettiest girl in class, all tricked out in her sparkly, jingly belly dancer outfit, with makeup on and her long, curly hair bouncing around. Talk about feeling like a dud. Yikes! I've never (since then) felt comfortable in costume, even though I designed and made them for many years.

When we moved to Duluth and bought the big old Victorian, it had been completely empty for eight lonely months. The neighborhood kids were circulating the story that it was haunted. They'd seen lights and heard noises. And so it was that it took several years before anyone under age 12 ventured up the long driveway on Halloween night, even though we offered the "big" candy bars.

Our kids had no such problem and were able to turn out the best and most imaginative costumes, using the findings in the big packing boxes left in the "haunted" attic, with maybe a little help from Mom. For instance, prom dresses, a Borgana fur coat, bathrobe, antlers, Ace bandages, sunglasses, draperies, and foam rubber sheeting became a fairytale princess costume (drapery fabric, some fake pink fur and sparklies); an elk (Borgana coat, antlers, button from the Elks Club and beanie with a chin strap to hold on the antlers); and the Invisible Man (completely wrapped in Ace bandages, including his face, wearing a bathrobe and sunglasses), and out they would go, usually with their snowsuits covering whatever they were wearing, because of course in Duluth, Minnesota, it almost always snows the day before Halloween. They would present themselves to the neighbors, unzipping and showing them, "Look! I'm a bunny rabbit!"

When we moved out into the woods, the driveway was a quarter-mile long, so the only Halloween-ers we got were our grandboys. They would storm up onto the back porch in their spotted dog (made by THEIR mom), Batman, and Underdog costumes and we would act surprised and try to guess who they were — followed by liberal offerings of the "big" candy bars.

But, I'm here to tell you that no place does Halloween better than A.T. Jones Costumers in Baltimore, Maryland. In addition to theater production rentals, Halloween is their big moneymaker; it is the place everyone goes for their costumes. So, they decorate for the holiday, have moving figures here and there to make unearthly noises, all appropriately scary. A true shopping immersion experience!

I constructed the hats and headpieces for the Baltimore Opera productions, in my basement workroom in Duluth and then shipped them to Baltimore. A.T. Jones, on Howard Street, pronounced "Hard Street," was where I would work when I got to Baltimore. The owner, George, had been a professional magician before taking over his wife's family costume business. Up on the third floor of this very old brick building on Howard Street was where he kept his mysterious props and costumes, and it was always dark up there. There were suits of armor waiting to jump on you, silk scarves wafting in any breeze, and lots of mirrors to make you think there was someone over there, watching, when it was really only you.

If you had to ride up the creaky, cantankerous, wooden freight elevator to retrieve something from the third floor, you always:

- Never went unless there were at least three or more things you absolutely had to have.
- Told someone where you were going and how long it was going to take you.
- Tried to take someone with you. Nooo, they all ran past you, shaking their heads- deadlines, deadlines! Where are all the heroes when you need them?

So up you went, all alone, into the mysterious darkness of disappearing victims, persons being cut in half and screaming "things" flying towards you. Okey, I probably imagined that last thing. As far as I know, no one ever perished up there. Oh wait, what about that one guy, Leonard? Went up to get all those Roman soldier helmets? Come to think about it, he wasn't there the next trip I made to Baltimore.

NOW THEN! A Halloween column originating in Duluth, Minnesota, would not be authentic without mention of "The Great 1991 Halloween Blizzard" that dumped 36 inches of snow on us, over a two-day period, beginning on Halloween afternoon. It's one of those folklore things. Most everyone was grounded at home for 4 or 5 days with no electricity. People remember where they were, what they were doing and most of all, what they couldn't do for four days, like turn on the lights, cook dinner, or make coffee. Some of us couldn't flush our toilets or take showers because we had wells with electric pumps.

  In our case, we had moved out to the log house in the woods the winter before. Tom came home early from work and said "storm coming." And it did! It came and came and came! Four days later, Tom snowshoed out to the main road (a quarter-mile, wading through the waist-high drifts) and was picked up by a friend on a snowmobile to get food.

Then, just at spooky midnight, came one of the prettiest sights I ever did see. Around the bend in our driveway trundled an enormous front-end loader, lights flashing like an unidentified flying object. The cavalry had come to plow us out! I swear I heard the "Lone Ranger music" playing. Really!

Chapter 20

THANKFUL FOR THANKSGIVING

"Over the River and through the woods, to Grandmother's house we go" always floats its way into my mind when I remember family Thanksgivings, because we did, indeed, go over the river- the muddy Susquehanna in Upstate New York, to be exact- to get to Thanksgiving celebrations at my Gramma's. The women would all be in the kitchen, each making their specialty to serve at dinner. My oldest Aunt made the creamed onions- dreadful, slimy things that my father thought were the best thing on the whole table. My mom was right up there with the shredded carrot/ orange Jell-O salad. Whoever heard of crunchy Jell-O?

The men would be in the living room, doing whatever men did before television and the all-day Football Marathon. The children (four cousins- the twins, me- the only child, and Sharel- everybody's favorite) were playing "Hide the Button." Really. I kid-you-not. Hide the Button. Having fun, too. After dinner, there would always be a "discussion" between my father and his sister- shouting and interrupting, posturing, and laughing. Those two loved to argue with each other, like a debate team event that they looked forward to every year. Everyone else just ignored them and went to clean up the kitchen. I never remember any leftovers. Except the creamed onions.

When my family moved to Rochester, Minnesota, one of the most amazing things we found was the "Thanksgiving Smorgasbord." Instead of piling all the food on the table and trusting that the turkey would get passed to you before all the dark meat was gone, you could just waltz right up there, get in line and take whatever you wanted…and then go back for more! In Rochester, the Carlton Hotel put on a Sunday smorgasbord that was legendary. It looked like one of those famous oil paintings that get made into puzzles. You know- the groaning board heaped with fowl and fish and split open melons, tipped-over wine glasses, (well, maybe not the wine glasses, it being Sunday in 1957) and all. But you get the decadent drift.

The first time we were invited to my husband-to-be's family, Thanksgiving was my first encounter with the lowly rutabaga. On the East Coast, we had turnips. In Minnesota, you have rutabagas. And I have to say, they are a vast improvement. Nothing's more divine than warmed-up rutabaga for lunch, the day after Thanksgiving. The other new experience with the Myers Thanksgiving was the raspberry sherbet, served right before dinner, in lovely little crystal stemmed goblets meant to "cleanse your palate." Didn't matter if the turkey was getting cold or the gravy lumpy, you ate your raspberry sherbet.

Several times after Tom and I and the kids moved to Duluth, we tried driving to Rochester to have Thanksgiving with our families, but the weather was never cooperative. The last time came as we were going over Thompson Hill, keeping an eye on the glaze of ice on the highway. I was knitting a pair of gloves for my dad, just to keep my mind off the road. There were cars in the ditch on either side, the kids were being very quiet, and the gloves were getting lumpier and more deformed. We started to slide and that's when we turned around and came home. Kentucky Fried chicken for Thanksgiving dinner never looked so good.

And so began the Duluth celebrations in the big old Victorian house. It was perfect for large, boisterous gatherings, no matter if the woodwork was being stripped or the wallpaper being peeled. The house always seemed happiest when a party was going on. Most years there were guests at the table- dancers, usually, because Thanksgiving falls right in the middle of Nutcracker rehearsals, when no dancer could even think of going home for a holiday. I remember one year, they taught us to play pinochle and another year the new puppy threw up under the dining table, complete with loud sound effects. The kids would compete to see who could stick the most black olives on their fingers before someone said, "Hey! Who took all the black olives?" There was one young man from out East who was so excited to have wild rice and said over and over how good it was, until I noticed he was eating the green bean casserole.

  Now that our kids are adults, everybody brings something and is also responsible for fixing it. Daughter brings the desserts and sometimes apps, too. Middle son brings the wine plus potatoes and rutabagas, which means peeling, chopping, cooking, and mashing them. Oldest son now brings the wild rice casserole and the Baileys, but for several years he contributed the turkey. He had friends from the Renaissance Festival who had free-range turkeys. One year he came with a worried look on his face and started by saying "Mom, it was the last one they had." "Okey," I said. He followed up with, "Not sure how we are going to cook it but I think it will be really good." "Okey," I said. He then concedes, "It weighs 55 pounds." Omigod! "There was a bigger one. 75 pounds, but it died of a heart attack just before I got there."

    We cut it in half with a Sawz-All, cooked half in the oven and half in the Weber. And mmm, yes, it was goo-ood.

Chapter 21

COLOR ME, COLOR YOU

I guess if people make up rules about something it just shows how important that something is to them. For instance, take color. There are all sorts of color rules that I grew up with, in the 1950s. You never wore red and pink together, nor green and blue. Christmas was red and green, Hannukah was blue and white or silver, Easter was pink and purple and you never wore white before Memorial Day nor after Labor Day. You just didn't. And lightning might strike you down if you wore brown shoes with a black suit. Period.

Your friend calls and says, excitedly, that they just bought a new car. Do you ask what kind it is? No. Do you want to know how many miles per gallon it gets? Of course not. "What color is it?" you ask.

Another friend was getting ready to paint her house, during the Covid quarantine. She went online several times to look at the color cards and chips from her local paint store, because the shop wasn't giving them out, at that time. She would then call with the color number she had chosen and order just a quart to be sure. The person who mixed the paint would meet her in the parking lot, as if it had become Black Market illegal to paint your house. She would go home, paint a good-sized patch, aaaand? It wasn't right. Didn't look like the paint chip. Back to the parking lot.

So many factors involved there. Her computer, her printer, the surface the paint was going onto, and the existing color of the trim next to the new color. Which way did that wall face, N, S, E, or W? Was the sun shining, was it a gloomy day? What color was the house next-door and was there any reflection? Quilters will often carry around miniscule swatches of fabric in search of the one they are looking to add to their project. They try to match the color exactly. Or, they try to pick up that tiny dot of purple printed on the fabric that you can only see if you have your nose right on it. I tell them, "Step away from the fabric! Stick it up on a wall and get at least 10 feet away from it. If you have a walk-out basement, go outside and look through the window. Put some other colors up there with it. See how it changes. Amazing, isn't it?" That's color for you.

I am not a scientist. You must have figured that out by now. The only reason I passed Biology in 8th grade was because I could draw so well. All those body pieces and parts. A+. But I have a rather bizarre color theory. Honestly, I know it's pure made-up Hokum, really I do. I know it's made up, because I made it up. And even I don't wholeheartedly believe it.

So, here it is: What if when you were just a little child, you and your mother were both looking at your blankie, and she told you that it was blue, because what she was looking at was what HER mother told her was blue. But what if it actually was green? What if the whole world saw green, but called it blue? I know- certifiable. But what if I'm right?

In two of my worlds, quilting and the theater, people can get awfully wound up about color, no matter what they're seeing. In quilting, a good 25% of quilters are unsure enough of their color sense that they have someone else pick out their quilt fabrics for them. I know because I have helped many people make those choices. It's my most favorite thing to do, actually. When we are finished, they almost always say, "I would never have put those colors and fabrics together." Why not? "I didn't think they would work," they say.

Of course they work, because the person I am helping actually put them together themselves, as we went along. I always have them go around the store or into their stash and pull out a piece of fabric that they just love. It doesn't even have to wind up in the quilt. But it shows me their gut feeling about colors. Then we work from that piece of fabric and gather our fabrics together. People have a hard time getting beyond the idea that someone else has to approve of their color choices or they might make a mistake. If they are pleased with the fabrics and colors, then they are right. No report cards

My first job was as an apprentice floral designer. We used to put together bouquets and put them in the cooler for the public to come in and buy. Uh-oh, here comes my boss. "All right! Who made the purple and orange arrangement, again? Claudia? C'mon, take it apart. Nobody will buy it. You NEVER use purple and orange together! It's a rule." So, defiantly, I made a purple and orange quilt, so many years later.

Color can grab you by the throat and yell in your ear. Color can lull you into a deep snooze. Color can set off almost any emotion and it's different from person to person. I once made a light but vibrant blue Sugarplum Fairy tutu for the Nutcracker. Yeah, yeah, I know she's always in pink. BUT, my costume designs, my blue Sugarplum. After watching the ballerina rehearse in it, seeing how it moved about the stage, I got a little teary. It was soooo pretty, it almost made your heart hurt. In my mind, I named the color "Heartbreak Blue." Nope, it's not in your big, big box of crayons; not yet, anyway.

And, speaking of the Nutcracker, the next chapter gives you the inside scoop of what goes on.

Chapter 22

INSIDE THE NUTCRACKER

It's Nutcracker Time Again. You may not have noticed all those little kids scurrying to get to the dance studios, like the tiny mice they might be playing. But the ever-patient parents, whose mealtimes and car pools now revolve around rehearsal schedules, have surely noticed. Their off-spring are now part of the Nutcracker tradition. The progression starts out with Mother Ginger's boys and girls, who spend their time shushing themselves and thinking up ways to make mischief, while concealed under the huge skirt of Herself, the big Mother. They come bursting forth and dance around her as she fans herself and looks aghast that she has birthed so many children. What was she thinking?

You may be surprised to learn that Mother is ALWAYS played by a man. A large, strong man, and not always a dancer. The costume usually weighs 60 to 80 pounds and involves harnesses. It seemed like every year we were reinventing Mother Ginger's costume. "She" was usually depicted as a large "trollop-y" woman with red frowsy hair and a big hat.

Making her tall enough to fit children under her skirt was always a challenge. We tried a rolling platform...nope. Drywall expanding shoes...nope. Two men-one balancing on top of the other...crash! Back to the drawing board.

After MG kids, the little "wigglers" graduate to mice, soldiers, and 1st Act party guests! The only thing better is to be one of the chosen ones to play Fritz, the ornery little brother, or Clara, his sister, whose growing pains and hero-worship of her "Prince-who-will-come-for-her" form the impetus of the whole Nutcracker story. It is indeed a heavy burden for a 10 year old little girl who also has to do her homework, wash her hair, feed her cat, and make sure that everyone she has ever known will come to see her *be* Clara. And please, please don't let her throw up on stage.

At this point, many little dancers decide to dedicate themselves and their parents' time and money to more frequent classes and, if you're a girl, "going on point" or if you are a boy, learning to jump, spin around, and land on your feet, all while hoisting a 75 pound, flailing body over your head. Others take up volleyball, join the rugby team, or decide to play the oboe. The young women who continue on are, to my mind, the most poignant part of the Nutcracker production: the Snowflakes. They are on point, they move gracefully and they don't run into each other. I challenge you not to get goosebumps when they swirl around, the chorus reaches its oo-oo---oo-OO-OO crescendo and the snow begins to fall. Yes, it's falling from canvas bags up in the fly space and yes, when those same dancers are off stage they walk into walls, drop all their stuff on the floor, and forget where they left their backpacks, just like normal teenagers, but for that one moment, they have gifted us with perfection. Goosebumps.

After that, the professionals aka "The Company" take over. It's 2nd Act, when Clara and her Prince (he who was miraculously transformed from the Nutcracker) are entertained by ethnic dances from all over the world. What you might not know is that every director/choreographer has the right to change the setting of his/her very own Nutcracker as long as the music and general storyline remain the same. Thus, we have had a Nutcracker set in turn of the century Duluth, one in Manhattan's Central Park , one with a Wizard of Oz-like black and white first act using on sale wedding dresses and rented full white tie and tails that - BOOM- exploded into full color for the 2nd Act. There have been ones with clowns, angels, Samurai warriors, and a dragon propelled by many small children. There have been some with and some without Snow Queens, bats instead of rats, and even one called "The Madcracker." My personal favorite characters are the four little shepherdesses with Marie Antoinette dresses and big straw hats, pulling sweet little lambs-on-wheels. A*dor*able!

So here come the big guns- Sugarplum Fairy and her Best Guy. They leap and pirouette and "trittsy" across the rubber Marley floor with their beautifully-arched pointy feet, all making you feel like it's the easiest thing in the world that they're doing and maybe you could do it, too, if only you got your momentum up. I will not <u>ever</u> forget the first time I saw the Prince do a stiff-armed lift over his head, one hand flat on the Sugar Plum Fairy's stomach. He was RUNNING full tilt, basically flying her around the stage like a paper airplane. Yes, it's lovely and entertaining when you see it on television, BUT when it's right there in front of you, done by the same people who would come every Sunday morning for waffles and asking if you could please sew on some buttons, it's OUTSTANDING.

    Many of the dancers I knew over a 29-year period have accomplished enormous success and are still performing or teaching, or running dance schools and companies of their own. Some have earned their professional degrees in other fields and are doctors, veterinarians, professors, actors and entrepeneurs. But the work ethic that they developed so they could learn the movements, convey the emotions, and push themselves to the wall is what helped make it all doable. All because when they were little kids they wanted to be a mouse in the Nutcracker.

Chapter 23

THE LEARNING CURVE

Most of the things that we know or know how to do, have been learned from other people. Our families teach us to talk, tie our shoes, and make scrambled eggs. They show us how to fish, to sew, to build birdhouses and how to do a reasonably good job of packing a suitcase. They tell us to make our beds, brush our teeth, do our homework and don't, for Heaven's sake, go out in public wearing what you've got on. "I don't care if every single one of your friends is wearing the same thing. Go upstairs and put more clothes on."

Your teachers try to tell you things and hope you are listening and interested enough to retain the information long enough to pass their tests. When was the Magna Carta signed? Who signed it? How many bones in your foot? How do you say, "Don't speak to the bus driver" in German?

Your friends like to tell you important stuff, like Joey Patterson is going to ask you to dance at the party on Friday night. You should hide. And you shouldn't wear that shade of lipstick; it makes you look like a zombie. If they're really good friends, they tell you that your breath smells like garlic. When you are older, they discuss how to keep the deer out of your garden, the best recipe for left-over turkey, and what do you do when your son brings home his new girlfriend and you take an instant dislike to each other. Your friends at work like to tell you where they went for dinner last Friday and what a dud the guy was that they were with. They don't think it's important to show you how to change the toner cartridge in the copy machine before they leave for the day.

  So much for learning life's lessons from others. What about stuff you learn from your own experiences, trial and error, good or bad? Will it stay with you longer because you experienced it or figured it out? Maybe.

  When I was about 3 years old, I took advantage of the fact that my mother was chatting on the phone to hide in the kitchen cupboard with spoon in hand and proceed to consume an entire jar of Hellman's mayonnaise. It was a large jar. I learned that not only does that much mayo make you violently ill, so that even looking at anything white and fluffy for the next ten years makes you break out in a sweat, but it also makes your mom really mad because it was in the middle of World War II and mayonnaise wasn't that easy to come by.

Some other things I learned the hard way by myself:

Just because you're new to the neighborhood, doesn't mean you should volunteer for everything you are asked to do, in an effort to look like the "good" new person. Why would you agree to be a Den Mother? What is your problem? Didn't you know you have to get your Cub Scouts to do the activities described in the handbook such as learning to tie knots, finding their way out of the woods, and earning their smudge-ridden fingerprinting merit badge? In my experience, they mostly confined their den meeting enthusiasm to learning to make things to eat, as well as eating them. I did learn that with a group of hockey-playing Cub Scouts you do not suggest making nut cups for the annual Cub Scout Banquet. Who knew?

I have learned to NOT rip off that temptingly waving, loose piece of ugly wallpaper, unless you are prepared to spend time and money taking off the other 310 square feet of it, none of which is the least bit unstuck.

If you are a computer person, you've already figured out at least two ways to get the computer to do whatever you want. Sometimes it involves reloading, uninstalling, deleting, and rebooting. Sometimes crying helps, too, with a whimper thrown in to bump up the urgency. Okey, I admit, the first time my computer "went down", I was taught to do those things by a nice young tech person. He did sigh a lot, but we got through it and this old dog used the new tricks I learned the next time the computer tried to get the better of me. Ha! And speaking of the treachery of the computer, haven't we all learned to check that we didn't accidently hit the "reply to all" button?

I have learned the hard and painful way that just because you could ride a bicycle as a kid and you were a whiz on the ice pond in your white Sonja Henie skates, there is no reason at all to think those abilities are still with you at 80, or even 50.

My grandmother, Toots, sewed on a Singer Treadle machine and at four years old I was just tall enough to rest my chin on the flipped-open top of the cabinet, so I could stand there for hours, watching her put little doll costumes together. My Gramma Clark spent several weeks one summer teaching me to embroider flowers and Sunbonnet Sues on pillowcases. My mom taught me to sew on her treadle machine for my 8th birthday and I immediately ran over my finger, requiring a trip to the Dr's office. So of course, I gravitated to a profession that required me to work on large industrial sewing machines that run at warp speed and make stage costumes with boning and buckram and hoops and ruffs. But I was prepared. I had learned to keep my fingers safely away from the flying needles. That's what I learned. All by myself.

Chapter 24

OH CHRISTMAS TREE!

My childhood Christmases were dark and warm, smelling of pine, as we opened our presents by the lights of the tree, which never appeared until early Christmas morning. Now that I've been through many Christmases with children, I am totally amazed that my parents pulled that off--waiting until the kid was asleep to quietly drag the tree in, set it up, and decorate it. No wonder I had to wait upstairs while my dad went down to make sure Santa had been there. Undoubtedly my mom was still struggling with the tree lights.

For years, my mom only decorated with blue lights, blue glass ornaments, and tinsel. Tinsel is like bagpipes--you are either a fan or not a fan. Tinsel should be one of the deciding factors in choosing a spouse, like the Miracle Whip vs. Mayonnaise question. Marriage is hard enough without having to argue about tinsel. Angel hair is not even to be spoken of.

Flocking. We were not flocked tree people. We never had a pink tree, nor even silver and I know people who will only have a Scotch pine or a fancy tree trucked in from the Great Northwest. We had plain old Balsam pines that would start shedding their needles as soon as you put them up, BUT they always smelled like Christmas. Oh yes! We also had bubble lights. They usually hung upside-down, like bats, and didn't work. So, it was always a big surprise when all of a sudden, they would start to bubble! Whoa! Who poked the bubble lights!?

Imagine my disbelief, our first Christmas, when I discovered that my bridegroom had been raised in a Scotch pine family with no tinsel! How had I not noticed that? At that time, I was working at a flower shop and had learned to make bows as big as your head. So, we got a Scotch pine tree and I decorated it with huge orange ribbon bows AND tinsel! Make it work, we said.

Then, came a military move to Germany for our little family, where Christmas is celebrated with much enthusiasm and often includes liquor-filled chocolate ornaments for the Tannenbaums. And yes, our two little boys had eaten most of them before I figured that out.

The late 1960s saw a succession of small trees jammed into the living room corner of our medical resident's housing unit, as we returned to Minnesota. The trees were dwarfed by the pile of toys for three children, dolls, bears, Legos, trucks, and pull toys that made dreadful noises. Wak-wak! Our tree was always up before Christmas morning--because -"Maaahhmmm, everybody else has their tree up. Santa won't even come if we don't have a tree!"

  Our first Duluth Christmas in the old Victorian house included plaid ribbons and sparkles covered everything! We had no furniture and all three children had the Chicken Pox. There they were, standing in front of the huge tree, wearing their first skis, wistfully gazing at the snow outside the windows. The house had 13-foot ceilings, which to me meant 12 ½ foot Christmas trees. One year, I exceeded the tallness limit and the marks were still on the ceiling when we sold the house.

  In the early '80s, my daughter and I went to the estate sale at the Bishop's House. Down in the cavernous basement was the specially made 30 pound rotating tree stand. $25! How could we leave it? BUT, we hadn't envisioned the effort and trouble it would cause. Now the tree had to be ramrod straight. If it was the least bit crooked, it wobbled like a guy on his 3rd bowl of Tom and Jerrys. But it was magical! When we built the log house, there was no question, THE TREE STAND came with us. We sold many things, but never that!

    The first Christmas in the woods saw us camping in the almost-finished house and the snow was getting deeper and deeper. In a burst of holiday cheer, Tom said " I think there are some good trees just behind the garage," and he trudged off on his snowshoes, returning with a large, snow-covered lump. We got it into the rotating stand and the snow began to melt. This tree had to be about 18 feet tall, with maybe 12 branches. We called it "Wilt the Stilt" and hung a few ornaments on it. Lights were too heavy and it would have taken many packages of tinsel to make it beautiful. After that Christmas we bought an artificial tree. Tom said he just didn't want to cut down anymore of *HIS* trees, even the ugly ones.

    The artificial tree had to be put together branch by branch. We devised a color code with ribbons to try to get it together in order. One year, we misplaced the list of colors and it wound up looking like a porcupine on a bad hair day.

    For years we grumbled about that tree and so, when we moved into our present home (the 1952 "Prairie Rambler"), we decided it was time to simplify our lives, so we sold **THE TREE STAND** and gave away the tree, with our blessings, Thank you, Bishop for all those years of magic.

Chapter 25

GOOD INTENTIONS AND LOFTY RESOLUTIONS

I've been thinking about good intentions and "meaning wells," as in, "she meant well, poor dear" and New Year's resolutions. I think they are all related and greatly overrated.

New Year's resolutions are sort of like campaign promises to ourselves. They sound so noble, so uplifting. We say just what we know we want to hear. But deep down they are really just so much hot air. Why is it we think we can ignore that two-pound box of Russell Stover's chocolates hiding in the cupboard? It certainly won't help with that 20 pounds we think we can lose.

Going to the gym and going to church are also biggies. We proclaim our resolutions loudly to our friends because they make us feel so "goody two shoes." Ever notice how quiet we become after missing four days lifting weights and instead spending several Sundays sleeping in?

Here's the answer! We should vow to do things we actually have a chance of accomplishing, like remembering to plug in our cellphones or putting out the garbage on the right day! I'm talking resolutions that would give us some positive feedback, instead of scolding ourselves for that maple nut ice cream. Yay me! Four days in a row I've remembered to make my bed! Yessss! I've gone a whole day without saying anything stupid and earning myself a "Motherrrrr!"

You know, sure as sunshine, you're only going to ride your exercycle three days in a row, then you are going to go back to piling your clothes on it, so make your resolution for only three days. See? That works!

Speaking of feedback, I'm going to take just a small detour here and climb on my soapbox. The first time most of us encountered feedback was on eBay. It seemed like a good idea at the time, letting the general public know if you had a bad experience or even a good one. Now, every time you go to a doctor appointment, hire a plumber, read a book, or purchase something from an online catalogue, you are expected to sit down and write all about the experience, whether it be wonderfully gratifying or horribly disillusioning.

To me, if I return to your business and buy something over and over, that's great feedback. If you never see me and countless others again, it should give you a clue that you'd darn well better check and find out for yourself what's going on with your business. However, I'm not going to bad-mouth you for the world at large to know about. Maybe you had a toothache that day. Maybe your cat died. Maybe the person packing up your orders has a new, dreamy boyfriend on the other end of her cellphone.

Whatever. When I was in junior high, we had something called a "slam book." Friends and not-really-friends would circulate these spiral notebooks with a name on each page and you were invited to give your anonymous opinion of that person. It was a rather cruel rite of passage and quite often hurtful but there it was, in writing, that nobody thought your jokes were funny and your eyebrows needed plucking. I think it was meant as encouragement to better yourself but more often than not, the criticism sounded like a judgement that might keep people from making friends and finding out what that person was actually like. Sort of like feedback, huh?

Sorry, I got off track. Resolutions. Question: Why do we only make them once a year or, with practicing religious folk, twice: one for the new year and one for Lent. When people make these firm statements about "no more pizza" or even "no more beer," they must know that they are only going to make it through the first week or so before their determination slinks off into the sunset and they feel bad about themselves.

So why not make a week-long resolution? "Wow, look at me, World. I went a whole week without eating the Butterfinger candy bar I know I have hidden under my bed!" See- there, a positive ending, not a negative. Or how about an everyday one? Hey! It's Tuesday! I exercised! Maybe for some, an hour-long resolution would do the trick.

Some people find it helpful to keep journals, as in, "Here, let me just write down that I have drunk 15 glasses of water today." But then, THIS happens. "Oh, Tom, sorry, I didn't have time to fix dinner tonight. I was too busy getting caught up with my lists, journals and feedback, but look at all the high-minded comments I've made!"

Or, here's an idea. You can just keep your resolutions and lists to yourself. Don't tell anyone about them. Make your list of resolutions and put it in that "safe place"- you know, the one you never can remember. That way, it will be easier, less embarrassing, and you won't feel so guilty when you find them and throw them away. Because you know you probably will. Plus, If you happen to be successful at any of them, you can always brag after the fact.

Chapter 26

FUNNY THING HAPPENED ON THE WAY TO A QUILT SHOW

You've probably heard that quilters are nice people. Kind, helpful, considerate and will share their last quarter yard of hand-dyed fabric with you. This is true, unless there is a quilt contest involved and they are one of the "involvees." Then they become Mama Bear, protecting and defending their quilted offspring.

I am a quilter- a competition quilter. I make my quilts to be entered into the many contests around the country, where they are juried into the finalists, or not; judged and given prize money and ribbons, or not. How did I get to be competitive? Who knows? I have no brothers or sisters. I never had to fight for the seat by the car window and I always knew who my mom loved best. Me, of course!

My husband and I had just built our log house in the woods. There was so much work yet to be done. We were living on an island of log on top of an ocean of dirt or mud, most of the time. We needed to plant stuff, make gardens, and break trails down to the river. We had planned to hunker down and read books for the rest of our lives if we got tired of being outside.

Along comes my friend, Jan, who had decided that now that I was retired from the theater costuming life, I needed to become a quilter, like her. What! Was she crazy? She invited me to go to the Minnesota quilt show with her, here in Duluth. Her cousin was visiting from Oregon and would be there. "I don't want to," I said. Jan: "Oh come on!" I replied, "No, I have stuff to do." Jan countered with, "You can meet my cousin." Oh, all right.

It's a well-known fact that quilting is an addiction and that seemingly innocent women (sometimes men), some looking like your dear old grandmother, love to spread this addiction, resulting in the fact that there are now well over 6 million quilters in our country (plus a few others who quilt but don't tell anybody about it). There are the hand quilters, the machine quilters, and even those who quilt on machines the size of your automobile. They make baby quilts, wedding quilts for their nieces and nephews, charity quilts to raise money, or just for comfort to people who are hurting. There are "show quilters," who enter the competitions in any or all of a dozen national quilt shows and earn or win impressive money and ribbons. Surprised? I was, too.

    When I first started quilting, a non-sewing friend asked me, "What are you going to do with all those quilts?" I answered, "Well, so far, it hasn't been a problem, I've only ever made three." But the fourth one was different. I made it at a quilt retreat. Other "retreaters" kept nonchalantly walking past my table and I could see them whispering to each other. What were they saying? Was there something the matter with my quilt? Oh noooo. WHAT was wrong with my quilt? Finally, one of them said, "You should really enter that in a show." "What do you mean, a Quilt Show? Well huh! You think?" And with that, the Competition Monster raised its ugly head and looked me right in the eye!

Chapter 27

TO SHOW OR NOT TO SHOW

The first show I entered was actually more of an exhibit...and surprise! My quilt was juried and accepted! It was held in the Goldstein Gallery at the Textile Department, University of Minnesota, in St Paul. My "Fire in the Rain Barrel" was "going to the show!"

At that time, at least in MY mind, there was "quilting royalty." That is, those people who were instrumental in the surge of innovative work in the 1970s and '80s. They made and still make quilts that grab you by the throat, shake you up, and yell, "LOOK AT ME, dang it!" It just so happened that this exhibit was hosting two of these immortals, And MY quilt was in the same show. Not only that, but, when I got to the gallery, I found that if I crammed myself up against the inside door frame and peered over my right shoulder, I could just get my quilt and one of the "Biggie Quilts" into the same photograph. Wowzer!

After that first show experience, I was all pumped up to enter my new purple and red

Bargello quilt into the local guild show. I arrive to turn in my artsy-fartsy abstract design wall hanging with the appliqued black tubes dripping silver beads, wild multi-colored backing, and imaginatively named, "Heart Throb." "Oh yes, thank you for asking, I WAS the one who had 'my work' at the Goldstein Gallery, last month. Yass. That was me." I was pretty obnoxious, I'm sure.

The next day, the show opened and I was right there to see My Quilt. Probably the star of the show, I thought. Uh oh, I couldn't find "Heart Throb!" Maybe they hated it and decided not to hang it. It was kind of weird. Maybe it broke some Quilt Police rule and was disqualified. How embarrassing! Finally, I spotted some familiar fabric and there it was! Hanging backside out! The hanging crew didn't realize the abstract Bargello front was the quilt. They thought the multi-colored fabric back was pieced. Well! You could practically hear my head deflate. Big lesson learned in competition-- if you can't be modest, for goodness' sake, be quiet about it!

I'd like to point out that it doesn't matter if you are competing in the Olympics or the hot dog-eating contest at the local tavern, you're going to have fans who think everything you do is great and you're going to have folks who actively dislike what you're doing, and will tell you so in their loud "outside" voices.

It was 1998. I designed and made a quilt I called "Passionflower," a diamond/pineapple with many shades of green, turquoise, coral, and gold. I used a couple of (Wow!) black and white animal skin prints for punch. It was a lot of color for then. It won the "Best Use of Color" award at the prestigious Pacific International Quilt Festival that year and even better, a friend and I were actually going to that show! Oh Boy! Was I excited! My first big award! It was a great show- lots of wonderful quilts, vendors, and exhibits.

So, there I was, gazing at my "Passionflower" quilt, admiring the ribbon and the big award sign, when an older couple came along. The woman looked at my quilt, studied the sign, checked out the ribbon and let out a snort. She turned to her husband and said in a loud trumpeting voice, "Best Use of Color? WHAT were they thinking?! Should be 'TOO MUCH Use of Color!'" and they chuffed away. Another lesson learned—DO NOT "lurk" around your entries at a show. You will always hear something you'd rather not know about. If I'd been over at The Ginger Cat booth, buying fabric, I would have never heard that. Serves me right.

Chapter 28

JUDGE NOT

I know that Judging is a terrible, rotten job even though I've never done it and never intend to. My friend, Shirley, was asked to judge a guild show in another state. It was one of those guilds where the same people have always won the big awards, so they expected that they always WOULD win the big awards. Shirley begged to differ and she did what they had invited her there to do- she judged the show. You would have thought she had declared that quilting would no longer be allowed in that state, there was so much hullaballoo about the winners and the losers. So Shirley, fearing for her very safety, quietly left her hostess' house in the middle of the night and drove 7 hours all the way home, before the show ever opened! She didn't even collect her hazardous duty pay! She never judged again, but then, they never asked her again, either.

    Judging is, after all, subjective! You have to know that for the most part, the Judge doesn't hate you or your quilt. Their comments are meant to contribute to your personal growth as a quilter. They don't "have it in for you." Unless, perhaps, your name happens to be glued onto that little cloth doll hanging in the judging room. You know, the one with the pins in it? Then you can worry.

If your quilt wins, you celebrate in some fashion and you dress up in your best "matches my quilt" outfit and stand in front of your prizewinner answering the excited questions from other quilters and letting them take pictures with you. What do they want to know? "How long did it take you?" Every dang time! Then, when you tell them three months, or six months or a year, doesn't matter, they ALWAYS say "Oh, I'd never have the patience!" As if they had been planning on rushing home to make this quilt themselves but now, because it would take so long, they just won't be doing it.

When it doesn't win anything and you get "skunked," you learn to suck up a big breath and say, "Oh y'know, it's just something I made for our bed." Then you try and paste that big fakey smile on your face. Because the next Judge may think it's the best thing to come 'round the bend in the last decade and give it Best of Show. You just never know.

So now I've got the answer for "what are you going to do with all these quilts?" I enter them into every single judged show they can go to. They travel the world in their little cardboard boxes, working their way, earning their keep, and sometimes bringing back cash money and fancy ribbon rosettes. At the end of their quilt show life span, when they have been hung, taken down, peered at, judged, written about, photographed, copied, patterned, packed, and unpacked a few bazillion times, they will retire, gracefully, into the quilt cupboard in my studio-out to pasture, making room for the up and comers. Aaaaahhhh. The life of a competition quilt.

Chapter 29

THAT ALWAYS MAKES ME LAUGH

My husband would tell our adult kids- "Find someone who makes you laugh".

Makes sense, but why do we laugh at what we laugh at? I always thought I had a pretty cerebral sense of humor, yet I chortle and snort at the Laurel and Hardy movie that shows them trying to move a piano from a 3rd story, narrow building. You just know the piano is not going to make it in one piece. But I know people who don't think Laurel and Hardy are the least bit funny. My husband and I have watched "The Producers" so many times (starring Zero Mostel and Gene Wilder), schmoozing little old ladies into supporting their flop Broadway musicals, and "Young Frankenstein" with Peter Boyle as Frankenstein, in his top hat and tails, doing the soft shoe. I will admit that "Laugh In" doesn't do it for me as much as it did 40 years ago, but "Pink Panther's" Inspector Clouseau driving his car into the lake for the umpteenth time starts helpless laughter. All pretty slapstick, if you ask me.

I'm with my friend Jan inside the fancy Minneapolis hotel elevator, visiting the Big City to celebrate our birthdays, and talking to beat the band. Finally wondering, after 10 whole minutes, why we weren't going anywhere. Huh! Hadn't punched the "up" button because we were talking so hard. Uh-oh. Try not to make eye contact with all those people waiting for the elevator.

During the same trip, we somehow set the timer on the TV. We'd click the "off" button, hop into bed, settle down, and the TV would blare back on. Get up, turn the TV off, hop into bed, settle, TV blaring. Over and over, until we were hysterically laughing and crying. We had to call room service to come up and turn off our television. How embarrassing!

I was at a quilt retreat where I was requested to bring a multi-plug to use. Everything was set up, machine, iron, light, but...dang! Nothing would go on. Check everything- yep, all "devices" plugged in. But nothing is working. Housekeeping came by and pointed out that I had plugged the multi-plug into the multi-plug. That's when you sneak a look around to see if anyone noticed.

FaceBook is a great source of hahahas- like the woman in bathing suit and rubber shoes, shower cap on her head, clutching her closed-up ironing board under her arm and charging into the ocean. The caption reads: "Ironwoman Contest."

Another one that reduces me to giggles is the big sheepdog seated at the computer, which shows a picture of a rowdy group of sheep. The caption reads: "Morty's been working from home, these days."

And finally, the "True Meaning of Dogsledding," as the two dogs race uphill in the snow, flop on their sides and shimmy down the icy hillside. Again, and again, and again. That's right up there with the backyard full of open cardboard boxes, each holding a cat. The caption is: "The Cat traps are working."

It's the opinion of a few people on Google that the humorous TV sitcom is dying. Why is that? Do we no longer think something that's funny is important? Are we so serious now, that we can't see the silly humor in Elaine and her "Big Big Salad". Can we ever say to someone, "No Soup for you!" without breaking up? Forget the gory crime shows and the ridiculous "Make it in the Jungle for a Week Naked as a Jaybird" shows. Just think about the final closer of The Mary Tyler Moore Show and the "Group Hug" as a clump of six sniffling people "group-shuffled" their way over to the desk for the Kleenex box. Hahaha! Which makes YOU feel better?

How about Tim Conway, tiring of the long-winded speaker, climbing up on the banquet table, pulling the tablecloth over himself, sticking his thumb in his mouth and gently dozing off? Or Carol Burnett, in the green drapery dress from a Scarlet O'Hara take-off, but with the curtain rods left in the shoulders? Or I Love Lucy and Ethel working in the candy factory, keeping up with the accelerating assembly line by stuffing chocolate creams into their mouths?

Tell me a "Sven unt Ole' Joke" and I'm your friend, forever. Cerebral? I think not!

Chapter 29

COVID EXCURSIONS

So, my question is----what's the first thing YOU'RE going to do when it is finally safe to go out and mingle with all the other "Quaranteeners?" My answer---I'm going to Bridgeman's for a hot fudge banana sundae. The kind in the tall milkshake glass. And yes: whipped cream, cherries, and waffle cookies, please.

It's been almost exactly a year since the everyday world as we know it came to a grinding halt. Many of you carried on and did the jobs that helped us maintained some semblance of normalcy. You worked from home or you continued to go out to work and hoped to be safe. I can count on my fingers and toes how many times this year I left my own property, BUT, my trips out were so memorable and enjoyable I thought I'd share them with you.

Last April, we'd only been "in" for a month, but my husband drove me out to Gordy's Greenhouse and let me wander as long as I wanted, sucking in the delicious warm plant smells through my mask.

June's special occasion was up around the corner, three days of trying to "socially distance" and stay out of the way, as daughter and family cleared out their house and packed the big moving van. A chance to see them all- sweet! But moving van- bittersweet!

July saw us (but mostly heard us) outside on our patio, listening to a jam session with bagpipes and didgeridoo. Strangely compatible. We are fortunate to have "in-house" pipers and friends with expertise in playing out-of-the-ordinary instruments. Thankfully, no one called the police and in fact, we heard clapping from the neighbors.

In August, our small lunch group of antique dealers decided to brave a visit to the Rustic Cafe, up the shore because we really, really needed pie. We sat 6 feet apart, at a large table, in a large room, trying to hear and understand "shop talk" mumbled through our masks. But the pie was worth it.

October was mostly cold and blustery, but one unexpectedly warm day, Tom and I went to Brighton Beach and sat, bundled up, on one of the wooden benches, immersing ourselves in the view and sounds of Lake Superior. All was quiet, with a family enjoying a last-of-the-year picnic a few rock outcroppings away. A solitary kayaker glided silently by. All of a sudden, WHOOSH! A diver popped up right in front of us, like a whale breaching the surface- full gear, wetsuit, mask, and all! We almost fell off the bench! Then with a swirl, he was gone. All quiet. Back to the lapping sound of the lake.

One Saturday in November, my quilter friend and I just couldn't stand it anymore, so she drove and we ran away from home. Shortest Road Trip Ever! We only got as far as our favorite quilt shop. Just what we needed—more fabric!

Thanksgiving and Christmas were solitary affairs. Instead of the exuberant family gatherings, there was just us two, trying to make the day seem as normal as possible. Brined the turkey, baked the pies, mashed the rutabagas, exchanged our gifts. All done by 2:30. Time for a nap. It helped that our kids all rose to the occasion and crafted their own holidays, each in their own way. One barbecuing out in the backyard, another had A Famous Dave's rib delivery and one doing a traditional

Christmas dinner, roast beef with all the extra stuff that goes with it.

The day out in late December was a drive to the Quik Trip parking lot in Floodwood, Minnesota, to exchange gifts with middle son and wife, all of us bundled up like little kids sent out to play in the snow. I doubt any viruses were able to penetrate all that wooly armor. Some "sort of" hugs and some chat through our icy clouds of breath and we were on our way back. Worth every mile.

This month's excitement was going to Sam's Club for our Covid 19 first shots. Did you ever, in your life, think we would be so elated and happy to be getting shots? Crazy.

Because, here's the thing, every one of those excursions, which in ordinary times would have been an everyday unremarkable outing, had the power to cheer and sustain us, to lift us and get us through that day, that week, that month, until the time comes when we hear the faint sound of the parade, coming from two blocks away. Humanity marching along, getting closer and louder, doing its' best to survive. I think I can taste that hot fudge, as we speak.*

*This column was written in April of 2021

AND THEN.....

A Few Anecdotes For Good Measure

"WHEN I'M RIGHT, I'M WRONG"

I drove the same Highlander for about 12 years, until it started making unnatural noises. I researched new and used Highlanders online to get an idea what was out there and available. I knew I didn't want one with the 3rd pop-up seat because, I reasoned, it took up extra cargo space. I was always hauling around antique furniture, rugs, and boxes and I needed all the space I could get. Wouldn't you know, every one of the new ones had that feature and most of the used, also. I was quite agitated about it and complained loudly to anyone who didn't run the other way. Why couldn't "they" carry a few without that dang seat?! What kind of customer service was that, blah, blah.

In cleaning up my present vehicle, I removed the cargo liner to vacuum underneath. "Hey Tom, what's this loop handle for?" So I gave it a hard yank. Up popped the third seat! Well, HUH....neverrr mind.

"SURPRISE!"

We were doing some renovating at the family cabin and had put a new floor in the kitchen, taking out the old wood cookstove and other things. We rented an enclosed trailer to bring the stove over to a friend of mine who had purchased it for his shop, and then pretty much filled up the trailer with old bedding and other disposables. We were in a hurry because it looked like there might be a storm coming, so we shut everything up and hit the road. Two hours later, we pulled into our driveway. There was no rain, but it was getting dark. We opened the back of the trailer and Holy Cow!!

A black lab puppy walked down the ramp, wagging her tail for all she was worth. We just stood there, stunned. We'd never seen her before. Tom turned to me, "Whose dog is that?" "Beats me!" sez I.

"STICKY BUSINESS"

Remember when sourdough pancakes and muffins were all the rage and everybody had a gooey bowl of sourdough starter in a warm corner of their kitchen? Yes. I did, too, and had made muffins for friends visiting from Grand Rapids that day. They enjoyed them so much that I made up a good-sized Rubbermaid container with starter in it and the instructions for them to take home. It was a cold day, but only a two-hour drive. I hoped the starter wouldn't be frozen to death on the way.

They were almost home, when he and his wife heard a large "boom" !!! as the top of the container blew off and the sweet-smelling goo exploded. Sticky, oozy sourdough starter, all over them and the inside of their nice, warm car.

"THE MINNESOTA FLAP"

Most quilt shows rely on volunteer help to get their event up and running, including one of the favorite jobs, which is hanging the quilts. There are volunteers who know what they are doing and volunteers who don't have a clue. My friend and I were going to the Minnesota Quilt Show, held that year in St. Cloud and to be honest, we might have fallen into the second category.

We got there early and thought we might as well help out, so we asked around, looking for a job. Somebody pointed us towards a few cartloads of quilts and told us to take them into the arena, through *that* door, and get them hung. They were part of a very special exhibit of a collection of antique hand-appliqued, hand-quilted quilts known as "Baltimore Albums." The person loaning this valuable collection to Minnesota Quilters was very protective of her quilts and expected you to be just as careful of her treasures.

In those days, Minnesota Quilters used what was known as "The Minnesota Flap." A wide strip of muslin was safety-pinned to the top edge of one quilt, then pinned to the top of the quilt that would hang on the other side of the free-standing pipe and drape. The only way to get the quilts in place was to fling them over the top of the pipe and adjust them. After a couple of hours, my friend and I were feeling pretty good about the job we'd been working on. We had almost all of the 25 large quilts hung and straightened. One last one to go.

I went on the other side to catch the quilt and pull it into place and my friend flung it over the 8 foot tall frame. Oh darn. Instead of going over, it was stuck on the top of the pipe. So, we started yanking on it to get it over. I KNOW you know what happened next. Yeah, it did. It happened. The pipe frame tilted and fell against the next one, and the next one and the next one. We stood and watched in horror, as the very special Baltimore Album Exhibit went down like dominos, in a tangle of pipes and muslin and hand-quilted quilts. It didn't stop until it got to the other side of the Arena.

We looked at each other. We really, truly wanted to run. We wanted to run, jump into the car, and drive home. But we didn't.

Thank you for reading my collection of stories. If you laughed a few times or a lot of times, that was my goal. If you loan it to a friend and tell them, "This is a good book, made me laugh," it has done what I wanted. If it makes either of you wish the second book would hurry up and be available, that would be the best.

My books are available on my website.

www.Claudiamyersdesigns.com

And in my etsy shop.

www.Claudiamyersdesigns@etsy.com

My second book contains another selection of Duluth News Tribune columns and a few extras. It is entitled "The Storyteller Rides Again", even if I don't …. Ride, that is. It will be available, soon.

Claudia's Bio

A former costume designer for The Minnesota Ballet, The Baltimore Opera and The College of St Scholastica Theater, Claudia is a competitive quilter and has won many awards at National Shows. Two of her quilts are in the permanent collection of the National Quilt Museum. In 2006 Claudia was named "Minnesota Quilter of the Year" and her quilting book, "A Passion for Piecing" is available through Amazon.com. She writes a column of humorous observations that appears twice monthly in the Duluth News Tribune. At her booth in Father Time Antiques, Canal Park, Duluth, she specializes in selling Persian and Oriental rugs. Claudia lives in Duluth, Minnesota with her husband, Tom, retired physician, now professional potter and their dog, Jordie. They enjoy spending time with their three adult children, their spouses, dogs and families. Claudia is currently at work on the next book in this series, tentatively titled "The Storyteller Rides Again".